CONTENTS

List of Diagrams		6
List of Tables		7
Preface		8
1	*The Urban Explosion*	9
2	*Europe: Land of Cities* The distribution of city sizes. Defining the city	10
3	*A Mobile Europe: Economy and Urban Expansion* Rural–urban migration. Migration and city growth. Foreign workers. City growth in eastern Europe. Other demographic constituents of urban growth. Movement into industry. The older urban–industrial regions. The industrial boom cities. The tertiary sector. Checking the growth of great cities.	25
4	*City Structure* Urban core and inner city. The middle zone. The suburbs. The rural fringe. City structure in eastern Europe.	42
5	*Community, Neighbourhood and New Structures for the City* Urban renewal. Structures for the suburbs. *Grands ensembles*. Building new suburban centres.	54
6	*Planning the City Region* Traffic in towns. Plans for metropolitan regions.	61
7	*An Urban Future?*	70
	Further Reading	71
	Notes	73
	Index	77

LIST OF DIAGRAMS

1 West European cities of 100,000 population and above, about 1950   11

2 City size distribution in western Europe   18

3 City size distribution in eastern Europe   20

4 France: *métropoles d'équilibre* and some other planning projects affecting urban regions   40

5 Structural elements of the City of Paris   45

6 The *Schéma directeur* of the Paris region   59

7 London and the Southeast: Abercrombie and after   66

8 Strategic plan for the Southeast, 1970   68

9 Structural elements of the Ruhr region   68

LIST OF TABLES

1 Estimated 1970 urban populations of some major world regions   13

2 The 30 largest cities of western Europe   14

3 Estimated proportions of total populations of European countries living in cities, 1970   16

4 European Community (the Six): distribution of employment by major sectors   25

5 France: migration by category of commune, 1954–62   28

6 European Community (the Six): foreign workers, 1970   31

PREFACE

This volume concentrates on western Europe defined as the original 'Six' of the European Community, together with the British Isles, Switzerland and Austria. Comparative reference is made to urban developments under the very different social and economic conditions obtaining in eastern Europe, defined as the states of Russian-style socialist type situated between western Europe, as defined above, and the boundary of the USSR. Limitations of space, and indeed of the author's experience, have prevented any serious references to developments in Scandinavia or in southern Europe, other than Italy.

Certain other areas falling within the general field of Urban Studies have necessarily been excluded. A section devoted to a comparative examination of housing provision in the various European countries rapidly showed signs of becoming a monograph in its own right, and the author was forced to conclude that so important a topic ought to be abandoned to an expert in this field. Similarly, it has not proved possible to say anything about the interesting question of the selection of appropriate areas of local administration in cities.

The author wishes to acknowledge the invaluable assistance of Miss Susan Rowland, Geography Laboratory, University of Sussex, who contrived the diagrams and drew all of them except Figure 3, which was drawn by Mr. Christopher Heaps.

T. H. ELKINS

University of Sussex,
1971

1. THE URBAN EXPLOSION

The city, and particularly the metropolis of a million inhabitants or more, is at one and the same time the place where European man lives his life of greatest intensity, reaping the highest material and cultural rewards, and the place where life can be at its most ugly and stressful, the environment at its most depressing. Most people in western Europe spend at least a few hours each day in the city, in an atmosphere polluted by noise, smoke and petrol fumes. Many workers choose to escape to sleep in the purer air of suburbs and satellite towns, but only at the cost of long daily journeys, and a twice-daily involvement with the urban transport system in its most immobile state. Those who remain to live in the central city have their own problems of life in a congested and often decaying residential environment.

At the administrative level, cities also suffer from lack of control over their own suburban zones, which send tidal waves of commuters to make ever heavier demands for expensive urban highways and transport systems. With city populations increasingly polarised between the very rich who can afford an exclusive central location and the very poor who cannot afford to move from the slums, city governments struggle to meet the need for urban renewal in an atmosphere of deepening financial crisis. Yet cities are also the points of decision, where the political and economic destiny of Europe is guided. They are the points of maximum intensity of exchange of ideas, magnets for the young migratory elite who will decide the future of Europe in the next half century. Can we ensure that the tensions of urban life remain creative and do not pass all bounds of human tolerance?

9

2. EUROPE: LAND OF CITIES

Anyone travelling the roads of western Europe will require little convincing that it is a land of cities (Fig. 1). A Midlander beginning his annual journey to the Mediterranean sunlight by way of the Channel ports will scarcely have left behind the 2.4 million inhabitants clustered round Birmingham before he is obliged to thread himself through the crowded Southeast region with its 17 million people, about 11.5 million of them in the Greater London conurbation at its heart. After a brief rest on the Channel ferry he will fortunately be able to leave on his left hand another 8 million or so people sprawling from the Nord region of France across the frontier into central Belgium, only to run almost immediately into much the same number of people concentrated in the Paris region. At least Paris will be less wearisome than the London region to traverse, since the converging motorways are linked by the peripheral boulevard, enclosing the 2.6 million densely packed inhabitants of the historic city of Paris proper. Once clear of Paris, however, the spaces between cities lengthen: there are 470 km (290 miles) before the one-million Lyon agglomeration slows progress towards the similarly sized Marseille region 320 km (200 miles) further on.

The alternative approach to the sun by way of the German *Autobahn* system and the Alpine passes would produce an even more urbanised prospect, for it follows Europe's main axis of city development, stretching from Merseyside to northern Italy. The way leads through the remarkable Netherlands *Randstad*, the circle of towns including Amsterdam, The Hague and Rotterdam which is inhabited by 5 million people, well over a third of the Netherlands population.[1] A mere 80 km (50 miles) further on and the Ruhr is reached; with its 5.6 million people, it is only a part of the Rhine–Ruhr concentration, which embraces cities like Düsseldorf, Cologne and Bonn to form a population concentration of 10.5 million, rivalling the London metropolitan area for

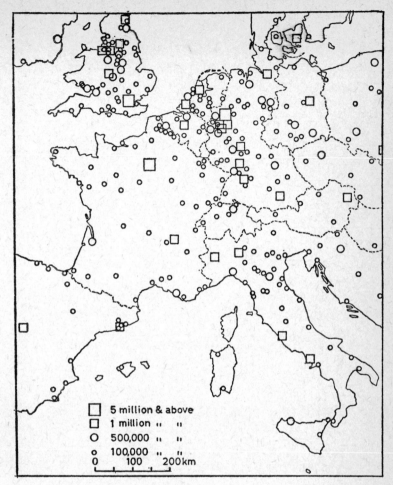

FIG. 1 West European cities of 100,000 population and above, about 1950

Source: Kingsley Davis (ed.), *World Urbanization 1950–1970,* vol. 1 (Berkeley: Institute of International Studies, University of California, 1969).

supremacy in western Europe. Three more great agglomerations must be passed, Rhine–Main (Frankfurt), Rhine–Neckar (Mannheim–Heidelberg) and Stuttgart until, beyond the cities of the Swiss plateau, the ascent over the Alpine passes to Italy begins.

11

It is of course equally true that our tourist could drive from the Midlands through Southampton and Cherbourg to the Mediterranean without passing through a single city of any great size. This reflects the almost precipitous falling away of city density from the Rhinelands into France and Spain (Fig. 1). There is a similar drop in city density eastwards and north-eastwards across Austria, northern Germany and Scandinavia. Until 1945 geographers would have drawn attention to a second European axial belt of cities, beginning on the Channel coast in northern France and southern Belgium, intersecting the main axis in the Rhine-Ruhr region, and continuing eastwards through Bielefeld, Hanover, Saxony and Silesia. While the first belt coincides broadly with the Rhine and its accompanying routes, the second corresponds with a great zone of overland routes linking Europe's principal coalfields. Today its significance is greatly diminished, partly because the lesser significance of coal in Europe's economy tends to be reflected in low urban growth rates, and partly because growth-generating traffic on the overland routes along this axis has been throttled east of Brunswick by the division of Germany. A glance at figure 1 will suggest that, away from these two axes, the few very large cities stand out as distinct islands of higher density. Typically they are either great national or regional capitals, like Paris or Vienna, or they are great seaport cities, like Marseille, Naples or Hamburg, or occasionally both at once, like Lisbon or Copenhagen.

It is not entirely a surprise to discover that western Europe's urbanisation is unique in the world. Only eastern Asia among major world regions has an absolutely larger total of city dwellers (Table 1). Admittedly, in the ranking of the world's largest cities, western Europe does not show up particularly well. There is a promising start, with Paris and London in the world's first six; indeed, if the Rhine–Ruhr complex of cities is treated as one unit, then Europe has three cities in the first seven. Otherwise the Ruhr, itself a group of cities, ranks only 17th, and for the fourth European city, the Birmingham–West Midland conurbation, it is necessary to descend to 36th place. There are only 16 west European cities in the world's first 100, and only about 30 with a million inhabitants or more (Table 2).

This rather modest standing of Europe in the league of really

Table 1

Estimated 1970 urban populations of some major world regions

Region	Total population (millions)	Urban population (millions)	Percentage urban
Western Europe[1]	263	183	70
Eastern Europe	124	65	52
Eastern Asia	920	292	32
North America	229	172	75
U.S.S.R.	244	152	62
Australasia	15	13	84
Northern Europe	22	15	68
Southern Europe[2]	75	37	50
Southern Asia	706	125	18
South America	189	107	57
Central and southern Africa	58	16	27

[1] Including Italy   [2] Italy excluded

Based on K. Davis (ed.), *World Urbanization 1950–1970,* vol. 1. (Berkeley: Institute of International Studies, University of California, 1969).

great cities has developed relatively recently, with the rise of giant cities in other parts of the world, first in north America, then in the developing countries of Asia, Latin America and Africa. However, the giant cities of developing countries are set in a preponderantly rural matrix of peasant villages and small market towns. By contrast the great cities of western Europe are the apexes of regular systems of urban settlements of all sizes, affording an urban way of life to an overwhelming majority of the population (Table 1). The peak of urbanisation is reached on the shores of the North Sea, where the United Kingdom, Denmark, Germany and the Netherlands approach or exceed 80 per cent urban (Table 3).

Yet, although a high proportion of urban dwellers is characteristic of western Europe, in this respect Europe is not unique : Australia, the United States and Japan have even higher proportions. However, in both the United States and Australia the spacing of cities is much more irregular than in Europe. The peripheral distribution of the great Australian cities is notorious. If the United States east of the Mississippi is more nearly equivalent to Europe, there is a vast area in the American West where cities are very widely spaced indeed. Japan is closer to western Europe in terms of city size and density, but the total population

13

TABLE 2

The 30 largest cities of western Europe

		Institute of International Studies 1970 projections		Various national calculations		
		Projected Population				Population
Rank	City	thousands	annual per cent growth	Date	Source	thousands
1	London	11,544	0·5	1971	CEN. E & W	7,379
2	Paris	8,714	1·8	1968	INSEE	8,197
3	Ruhr (*Rhine–Ruhr)	6,789	2·0	*1967	C. EUR.	10,412
4	Birmingham	2,981	0·7	1971	CEN. E & W	2,369
5	Rome	2,920	3·8	1966	SVIMEZ	2,725
6	Manchester	2,541	0·1	1971	CEN. E & W	2,387
7	Hamburg	2,407	1·1	1967	C. EUR.	2,088
8	Glasgow	2,008	0·2	1971	CEN. SCOT.	1,728
9	Leeds–Bradford	1,945	0·1	1971	CEN. E & W	1,726
10	Stuttgart	1,935	2·7	1967	C. EUR.	2,014
11	Vienna	1,890	0·1			
12	Liverpool	1,823	0·5	1971	CEN. E & W	1,262
13	Cologne	1,788	2·7	*(see Rhine–Ruhr)		
14	Milan	1,750	1·6	1966	SVIMEZ	5,211
15	Rhine–Neckar	1,578	1·6	1967	C. EUR.	1,101
16	Munich	1,502	1·5	1967	C. EUR.	1,463
17	Frankfurt	1,452	0·5	1967	C. EUR.	2,375

18	Naples	1,300	1·1	1966	SVIMEZ	3,517
19	Düsseldorf	1,264	2·9	*(see Rhine–Ruhr)		1,074
20	Lyon	1,226	4·0	1968	INSEE	1,060
21	Rotterdam	1,222	4·0	1968	C. EUR.	804
22	Tyneside	1,193	0·3	1971	CEN. E & W	1,494
23	Turin	1,175	2·0	1966	SVIMEZ	1,046
24	Amsterdam	1,139	2·3	1968	C. EUR.	964
25	Marseille	1,061	3·4	1968	INSEE	
26	Wuppertal	1,032	1·5	*(see Rhine–Ruhr)		1,077
27	Brussels	1,014	0·9	1968	C. EUR.	728
28	Hanover	931	0·8	1967	C. EUR.	1,124
29	Genoa	930	2·0	1966	SVIMEZ	795
30	Nürnberg	852	1·5	1967	C. EUR.	

NB: The statistical city figures of the Institute of International Studies are not strictly comparable with the various national calculations, which are also not strictly comparable with each other.

Sources: K. Davis (ed.), *World Urbanization 1950–1970*, vol. 1 (Berkeley: Institute of International Studies, University of California, 1969).

The additional national calculations are derived as follows: CEN. E & W = UK, Office of Population Censuses and Surveys, *Census 1971, England and Wales, Preliminary Report*; CEN. SCOT. = General Register Office Edinburgh, *Census 1971, Scotland, Preliminary Report*; C. EUR. = Council of Europe, *European Conference of Ministers Responsible for Regional Planning*; CMAT 70/3–4, Strasbourg 1970; INSEE = L'Evolution de la Population au Niveau Régional et Urbain, 1962–68, *Les collections de l'Insee* D1; SVIMEZ = S. Cafiero and A. Busca, *Lo Sviluppo Metropolitano in Italia* (Roma: SVIMEZ, 1970).

TABLE 3

Estimated proportions of total populations of European countries living in cities, 1970

Core countries of western Europe	%	Countries fringing western Europe	%
West Germany	82	German Democratic Republic	84
United Kingdom	79	Denmark	80
Netherlands	72	Sweden	60
Belgium	69	Spain	59
France	68	Poland	56
Luxembourg	66	Norway	55
Switzerland	60	Czechoslovakia	52
Italy	52	Hungary	43
Austria	51	Jugoslavia	39
Ireland	51	Rumania	39

Source: K. Davis (ed.), *World Urbanization 1950–1970,* vol. 1 (Berkeley: Institute of International Studies, University of California, 1969).

is much less. West European urbanisation offers a unique combination of a very high proportion of the total population living in towns, of a very large total urban population, and of a dense concentration of towns of all sizes into a relatively restricted part of the earth's surface.

It will be apparent from Table 1 that eastern Europe stands at a lower level of overall urbanisation, although in fact the area is advancing quite rapidly in the same direction as western Europe. There are, however, great internal contrasts, with the DDR at one extreme having the same intensity of urbanisation as the countries surrounding the North Sea, while in Jugoslavia, Rumania and Bulgaria the proportion of population living in cities is still quite low.

There are, however, significant differences between the various east European countries (Fig. 3). Only in the DDR and Poland is the largest city supported by anything approaching a regular system of regional capitals at around the $\frac{1}{2}$–1 million mark.[2] Significantly these are both countries which emerged, in whole or in large part, from what was formerly the territory of the highly urbanised German Empire. Elsewhere the general pattern is of the utter primacy of the capital city, a situation which is generally characteristic of developing countries. Even in Czechoslovakia, with its distinct Czech, Moravian and Slovak components, Prague is the only really great city: Brno and Bratislava are not on the scale of the provincial centres of Poland or the DDR. The same may be said of Rumania, where Cluj and Iaşi cannot in any way rival Bucharest. In Bulgaria, the centralised planning of economy and society has caused Sofia to outgrow vastly all former rivals. Centralisation is most pronounced in Hungary, where Budapest maintains the scale and predominance that it developed before 1918, when capital of a territory far larger than Hungary today. Jugoslavia offers yet another variation: the composite origin of the country and its present federal structure are reflected in the existence of a number of important cities, one of which, Zagreb, closely rivals Belgrade in size.

THE DISTRIBUTION OF CITY SIZES

In Figure 2A a graph has been made of west European city populations of half a million and above. City size is expressed on the vertical axis, and the ranking of city by size on the horizontal axis. The most obvious feature of the graph is the overwhelming predominance of the two great national capitals, London and Paris, followed by the Ruhr conurbation. These tower above the remaining large cities, which arrange themselves into a neat and gentle curve, suggesting that western Europe is at this level of size provided with a neat and orderly system of great cities of all sizes within this range, without any further breaks or discontinuities. If the same cities are plotted on a logarithmic scale (not illustrated) they arrange themselves in a 'straight line with a slope approximating to —1', a statistical condition held by a number of writers to indicate that the area concerned has a completely developed system of cities of all sizes.[3] Yet Paris, London and the Ruhr still stand far above the general range, as altogether extraordinary in their population size.

When west European countries are looked at individually much of this orderly sequence disappears (Fig. 2B). City size distribution varies markedly from one country to another. One of the most striking contrasts is between West Germany and France. West Germany, deprived of its former national capital in Berlin, has a characteristically strong development of a group of cities in the 1–2 million range. These are the great regional

17

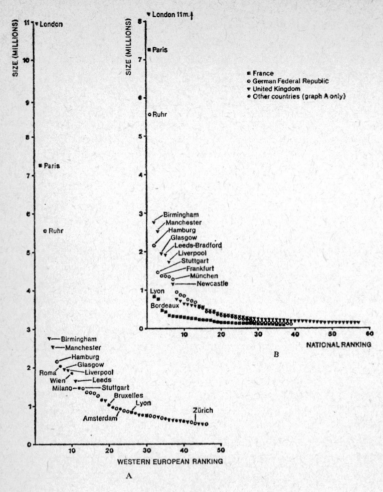

FIG. 2A, B City size distribution in western Europe

Source: Kingsley Davis (ed.), *World Urbanization 1950–1970,* vol. 1 (Berkeley: Institute of International Studies, University of California, 1969).

capitals of a country where national unity is a relatively recent creation, and which today has a federal constitution. France, with its centuries of unity and strong tradition of centralisation, could not be more different. Here there is a vertiginous plunge from the 8 million of Paris to Lyon at only the million mark, this city and possibly Marseille being the only French cities to approach the importance of the German or Italian regional capitals. Figure 2B shows how the curve of French city size continues to plunge steeply until, at about 300,000, it flattens at a generally lower size level than the curves for Germany and the United Kingdom. The characteristic French lack of really large cities other than Paris also comes out clearly on the map of west European cities (Fig. 1); the contrast with the range of cities encountered in the Rhinelands is immediately apparent.

The United Kingdom, as ever, stands somewhere between the two extremes. Centuries of national unity are reflected in the predominance of London, but a lesser devotion to centralisation and the effects of the Industrial Revolution have rendered the primacy of London less extreme than that of Paris. There is a substantial intermediate group of great cities in the 1–3 million range on the coalfields of the Midlands and the North which are generally bigger than even the German regional capitals (although typically much more stagnant in their population growth). Clearly these differences in city size distribution reflect changes in historical development, but they are also of current social and economic significance. They indicate why in the United Kingdom the government has for 30 years been concerned to check the growth of Greater London, why in France there is so much concern with the manner in which the growth of Paris has drained the vitality of the rest of the country, and why these preoccupations are hardly felt in Germany, with its balanced equipment of cities of all sizes.

Cities in eastern Europe are, in general, of modest size. At about 1960 there were only six with over a million inhabitants (as compared with 25 in western Europe) and only another five in the $\frac{1}{2}$–1 million category. Berlin, its largest city, is a victim of political geography, internally divided and stultified in growth. After Berlin the largest agglomeration is provided by the Katowice–Bytom–Zabrze group of cities in the Upper Silesian industrial region of Poland. The largest 'normal' cities are two national capitals, Warsaw and Bucharest. Taking east Europe as a whole, however, there is none of the crushing predominance in size that London and Paris exercise in western Europe. The general trend of the rank/size graph of the cities of eastern

19

Europe suggests that the largest cities are, if anything, rather smaller than might be anticipated (Fig. 3).

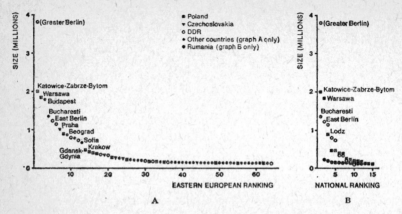

FIG. 3A, B City size distribution in eastern Europe

Source: Kingsley Davis (ed.), *World Urbanization 1950–1970*, vol. 1 (Berkeley: Institute of International Studies, University of California, 1969).

DEFINING THE CITY

Hitherto it has been assumed that the meaning of the term 'city' is self-evident, but it is in fact far from easy to arrive at an acceptable definition. *Webster's Third New International Dictionary* tells us that the city is (among other things) 'a populous place: a place larger than a village . . . a large, prominent or important center of population . . .' Just how large a 'place' has to be in order to be a town or even a city (current English usage provides no firm dividing line between the two terms) is in the first instance a matter of official definition by governments. For Ireland the lower limit of what is deemed to be an urban settlement is as low as 1,500; in western Europe it is generally around 2,000, while the Netherlands, Austria and Switzerland have higher minimum figures. Rather characteristically the United Kingdom has no fixed minimum, but states that an area is urban if declared to be so for administrative purposes, that is, if it is accorded the status of county borough, municipal borough or urban district. Clearly the United Kingdom is a law unto itself, but in western Europe as a whole, as on a world scale, there is a surprising amount of agreement that the point at which settlement is deemed to be urban lies somewhere between 2,000 and 7,500 minimum population.[4]

Differences in national definitions of what is considered urban are not necessarily the result of mere chance; they may reflect objective differences in patterns of settlement. Countries such as Ireland, where the rural settlement pattern is one of dispersed farmsteads associated with small towns that provide basic services, will tend to set the urban limit low. Countries where farms are characteristically grouped into large villages will set the figure high in an attempt to distinguish village from town; 5,000 is a figure commonly adopted, for example in the Netherlands. However, setting the figure high presents its own problems, as in France, where a lower limit high enough to prevent the large villages of the north from being classified as urban will exclude the *bourg*, the small urban centre of 1–5,000 inhabitants which, especially among the dispersed farms of the south, forms the lowest member of the urban hierarchy.

To deal with this problem many countries introduce other criteria into their definition of what is considered 'urban'. The Netherlands adds to its clusters of a minimum of 5,000 population also those communes where not more than 20 per cent of the economically active males are engaged in agriculture. Italy requires that the agricultural proportion should not exceed 50 per cent.[5] What makes a place urban is not merely the assemblage there of a certain number of people. What they do there, the functions on the settlement concerned, are also significant.

The problem of setting an acceptable lower limit to what is considered to be urban does not produce any great difficulties in the context of the present study which, being on a European scale, must necessarily concentrate on the larger cities. Of much more immediate concern is the problem of fixing an outer limit to the city, of deciding exactly how many people live in it. It is a fairly familiar experience that the population figures given in the reference books for Europe's cities as defined for administrative purposes give little indication of their true extent. It has rarely proved possible for the extension of the city's political boundaries to keep pace with the urban explosion of the last 150 years. A familiar example is provided by the city of Paris, which stands in the statistical reference books as having a population of 2.6 millions. In fact the 'real' population of Paris, of people who live in the continuously built-up area of the Paris agglomeration, is over 8 million.

In western Europe, readiness to adjust boundaries to urban growth appears to vary from one country to another. In France, communal boundaries, including city boundaries, have remained remarkably static throughout all the city growth of the last 150 years, and in particular through the explosive expansion of the last quarter century. Accordingly, the political city boundaries are drawn very tightly, and the proportion of the true or statistical city population living in the core city is low. Rouen, for example, appears to have only about a third of its statistical city population living within its constricted political limits; even its modern university has been forced to seek a site in a neighbouring commune. By contrast, German cities appear to have experienced less difficulty in extending their administrative limits as they grew, so that for German cities like Munich or Hanover, standing alone without the complications that spring from being set in an urbanised tract or conurbation, the population resident in the politically defined core may be about 80 per cent of the total population of the statistical city.

Eastern Europe presents, if anything, even greater difficulties of urban definition. There are many settlements which are traditionally and legally recognised as towns, but which have remained relatively unaffected by industrialisation. Poland in 1960, for example, had 172 towns with fewer than 3,000 inhabitants, including four with fewer than 1,000. In the majority of these small towns agriculture was the most important single occupation, and in 15 of them the proportion of the work force engaged in agriculture exceeded 50 per cent. On the other hand, industrialisation has created many new residential areas which are neither rural nor legally recognised as towns. A particularly difficult situation exists in Hungary where, for historical reasons, settlements of 20,000 inhabitants or even more grew up which were essentially agricultural in nature. This makes it very difficult to fix an appropriate lower limit for what is considered to be urban. One consequence of this situation is that, in spite of considerable post-war industrialisation, the proportion of people considered to be urban in Hungary has not increased very much. Undoubtedly there has been massive urbanisation, but it has tended to take the form of the functional transformation of these swollen agricultural settlements. Numerous examples can also be found of the usual slowness in adjusting city boundaries to population growth. Boundaries appear to have been particularly tightly drawn in Czechoslovakia, where Prague and other cities do not fully include their surrounding suburbs and commuter villages.[6] On the other hand, the further southeast one goes in Europe, the more generously at least the capital cities appear to be defined. Bucharest, Belgrade and, above all, Sofia stand in widespread capital territories. Comparisons of population figures for the cities of eastern Europe must therefore be made with care.[7]

The French, spurred no doubt by the glaring inadequacy of any figures based on their politically defined cities, have been leaders in the development of new statistical definitions of their cities. They have used the basic unit of the commune (there are nearly 38,000 of them in France) to build up 'urban agglomerations' of 2,000 people or more. The inclusion or otherwise of communes on the fringe of the agglomeration is decided on the evidence of the continuity of urban development as shown on maps, air photographs and, if necessary, in ground survey.[8] At the 1968 census there were in France 726 agglomerations of communes and a further 657 single communes having 2,000 inhabitants or more, in all containing two-thirds of the population of the country.

Among other countries to advance along similar lines are Switzerland,[9] Italy[10] and Belgium. Britain takes the more limited step of specially defining six conurbations, in addition to Greater London. Germany rejoices in three separate definitions, 10 very extensive *Ballungsgebiete*, 25 more narrowly defined *Verdichtungsräume*[11] and 68 city-regions (*Stadtregionen*).[12]

These attempts by the various European countries to develop a statistical city definition were developed independently for purely internal needs, and so lack strict comparability, but they give a more valid impression of relative city size than do the politically defined core-cities alone (Table 2). Fortunately an independent check is provided by the calculation of populations of cities over

100,000 undertaken by Professor Kingsley Davis of the Institute of International Studies at the University of California, Berkeley.[18]

But the city is more than an assemblage of bricks and mortar, or of resident population. To quote Webster again it is also 'a relatively permanent and highly organized center having a population with varied skills, lacking self-sufficiency in the production of food, and usually depending primarily on manufacture and commerce to satisfy the wants of its inhabitants. . . .' These things are less easy to confine within a single continuous boundary than the physical agglomeration, but they are no less essential to the urban definition. Some of the economic aspects of the city may indeed involve world-wide relationships. This is especially true of the great financial centres, London or Zürich, or the world ports, like Rotterdam or Marseille, receiving food and raw materials from the ends of the earth, to be paid for in manufactured goods and commercial services. Other urban activities have a more local outreach: the town as a 'central place' provides a 'sphere of influence' of surrounding territory with shopping facilities, economic organisation, public administration, public services of all kinds, newspapers and other forms of communication. Given modern forms of suburban rail and road transport, the town's workers may also live far out in the surrounding countryside. The existence of these flows of services out from the city, and of commuting workers into it, make it impossible to think of the city today as in all respects limited to the agglomeration, the statistical city, however widely defined. Cities have become organising centres for vast tracts of surrounding countryside, their radiating influence increasingly dissolving the formerly sharp division between urban and rural society.

3. A MOBILE EUROPE:
ECONOMY AND URBAN EXPANSION

RURAL–URBAN MIGRATION

The last quarter of a century has seen sweeping changes in the way that west Europeans earn their livings. Most obvious has been the sharp decline of those engaged in agriculture (Table 4). The six founder members of the European Community shed $6\frac{1}{2}$ million people from their agricultural work force in the period 1958–70.[14] Developments in eastern Europe have been no less dramatic.

TABLE 4

European Community (the Six) : distribution of employment by major sectors (per cent)

Sector	1955	1960	1965	1970
Agriculture	24.3	19.6	15.9	13.4
Industry	40.0	42.4	43.5	43.9
Tertiary	35.7	38.0	40.6	42.7

Source : Commission of the European Communities *Preliminary Guidelines for a Community Social Policy Programme*, Paper Sec (71) 600 Final (Brussels, 1971).

Leaving agriculture as an occupation does not necessarily imply deserting the countryside as a place of residence. In places where cities are thickly scattered, it may be possible to travel to a new place of work without leaving the family house, particularly now that the motor vehicle is available to enhance individual mobility. There are in any event some parts of Europe where industrial employment has long been combined with part-time farming on small family holdings.[15] Under modern conditions of industrial prosperity and a relative depression of agriculture the worker-peasant increasingly tends to abandon his holding, while keeping on the farm house purely as a residence. He may use scraps of his fields to build houses for his children, or for letting or sale to others. Gradually the village turns into a working-class commuter settlement, an extension of urban life into the country-side. Such settlements are characteristic of Hessen, northeast Bavaria, Switzerland, southwest Germany, the Czech lands, parts of eastern France and the Low Countries.

However, it must be accepted that most of those who in their active years leave agriculture as an occupation are obliged sooner or later to take the road to the urban areas, especially if they live outside Europe's main axial belt of cities.

MIGRATION AND CITY GROWTH

A closer idea of rural–urban movement can be gathered by an examination of the situation of France where, with the exception of a brief 'back to the land' movement in the depression years of the 1930's, the proportion of the work force engaged in agriculture has fallen steadily from 45 per cent in 1906 to 27 per cent at the 1954 census and 15 per cent in 1968.

In the intercensal period 1954–62 French agriculture lost the extraordinary total of 1,247,000 workers, a rate of decrease of 3.5 per cent per year. This loss was reflected in an absolute decline in the total number of employed persons in 13 of the 21 French planning regions, situated predominantly in the rural west. In no fewer than 17 of the 21 regions there was a net loss of active population through outward migration. By contrast, the highly urbanised Paris, Rhône–Alps and Provence–Côte d'Azur regions showed a marked increase in their actively employed populations.[16] In terms of total population this meant that 3.3 million people or 7.1 per cent of the total population moved from one planning region to another, to the net advantage of the more urbanised regions as already noted. But the number of persons changing their department of residence was 4.9 millions, and no fewer than 12 millions changed from one commune to another. It would appear that most migratory movements, including presumably rural–urban movements, were of relatively short range.[17]

An examination of these movements by category of commune tends to confirm this view. Rural communes were characterised by a high rate of emigration, on balance contributing over a million people in 1954–62 towards the building up of urban

France (Table 5). The more purely rural and agricultural the commune, the greater the proportionate loss.

The smaller urban agglomerations below 5,000 inhabitants appeared to be in a whirl of movement, receiving a quarter of their population from rural areas but passing an equivalent number of people to larger agglomerations. Each and every category of agglomeration except for the culminating peak of Paris took in population both from rural areas and from agglomerations in lower categories, but lost population to all higher categories including Paris.

There is thus a good deal of evidence that the first move after leaving agriculture as an employment is likely to be a short one, to a nearby small town. Far more rural people went to towns under 100,000 in population than moved to the Paris region and the other large agglomerations of 100,000 and above. What then happened was a great shuffling up the urban hierarchy. At the peak of the hierarchy, the Paris region gained on balance far more from the other towns of France than from direct rural–urban migration.

It is very easy to be impressed by the dominance in European social geography of the large agglomerations, spreading ever further over the landscape, and to assume that they are the principal targets for migration, now as in the recent past. The evidence of France in 1954–62 does indeed show that 60 per cent of the increase by migration went to the large agglomerations and the Paris region. It was, however, the towns in the 50–100,000 category that retained the greatest proportionate share of migrants. Whether towns in this category are showing a similar migration growth in all parts of France, or whether we are seeing here rather the spreading out of existing conurbations into medium-sized agglomerations on their periphery, is something that will require further investigation.

In the subsequent 1962–68 period French agriculture lost a further 800,000 employed persons which, in proportion to the already reduced numbers in this branch, represented an even higher rate of loss than the 1,247,000 of the previous intercensal period. It would seem that in absolute terms the contribution of agriculture to the rise of French cities has passed its peak. In addition the efforts of the French government to build up industrial

27

TABLE 5

France: migration by category of commune, 1954–62 (thousands)

Category 1962	Proportion of total population %	Immigrants by category of commune in 1962	Emigrants by category of commune in 1954	Migration balance	Percentage change 1954–62		
					by immigration	by emigration	migration balance
Rural communes	38	1,350,5	2,416,4	− 1,065,9	8,0	13,5	− 6,4
cities and urban agglomerations:							
Less than 5,000	5	537,2	518,4	+ 18,8	24,7	24,1	+ 0,9
5,000— 9,999	5	504,7	452,7	+ 52,0	24,5	22,6	+ 2,5
10,000—19,999	4	453,1	388,0	+ 65,1	23,9	21,2	+ 3,4
20,000—49,999	7	698,4	576,0	+ 122,4	21,8	19,4	+ 3,9
50,000—99,999	6	556,6	399,8	+ 156,8	20,8	15,9	+ 5,9
100,000 and above	19	1,232,7	878,2	+ 354,5	14,3	10,7	+ 4,1
Paris agglomeration	16	889,8	593,5	+ 296,3	12,2	8.5	+ 4,1

Source: M. Schiray and P. Elie, 'Les Migrations entre Région et au Niveau Catégories de Commune de 1954 à 1962', Les Collections de l'Insee D4.

employment opportunities outside Paris have undoubtedly had their effect, especially in western France. Only one region, Limousin, registered an actual decline in active population, although as many as sixteen regions lost more workers by migration than they gained. The retention of active population in the more rural planning regions, particularly those of western France, did not of course mean that the movement to the cities was checked, but rather that more employment opportunities were being found in the cities within the regions concerned. Even so, the highly urbanised Paris, Provence–Côte d'Azur and Rhône–Alpes regions were still the principal destinations of those workers whose migrations took them beyond their regions of origin.[18]

Italy obviously falls into the same category as France, but the draining of workers from agriculture is less complete and the rate of movement still very high; nearly 3 million people between 1958 and 1969. This movement out of Italian agriculture has translated itself into massive rural–urban migration, including long-distance movements from the Mezzogiorno to the cities of northern Italy, Switzerland, France and Germany. Between 1952 and 1966, 4.7 million people left the rural areas and the small towns of Italy. There was a corresponding migratory rise of nearly 3 millions in the population of the country's city regions. Rome accounted for over half a million of the increase, and virtually all the remainder went to city regions north of a line from Ancona to Livorno.[19]

Germany is a special case. Between 1950 and 1968 the numbers employed in agriculture dropped from 5.2 millions to less than 3 millions, bringing the proportion of the active population in this sector to below 10 per cent. The rural–urban migration consequent on this change was, however, caught up in the much vaster movement to the cities of the wartime evacuees and refugees from lands to the east, who at the end of the war had found shelter in rural areas.

A massive drain of population from rural areas outside commuting radius of the cities went on until 1956. From then until 1961 the rural areas still had a small loss by migration, but on balance a small increase of total population, although not one to be compared with the rate of increase of the city regions. The further the rural areas were from a city, the greater the population losses by migration, until a few of the most remote areas of all still registered an absolute decline.[20]

The far end of the spectrum is provided by the United Kingdom. Agriculture has continued to lose workers, but absolute numbers are so small that the overall effect is lost in the diffusion of commuter populations outwards from the cities. So far from the rural areas providing migrants to nourish urban growth, they are proportionately the most rapidly growing parts of the country, adding 1.62 million people to their population in the decade 1961–71. Presumably this is a situation towards which the less urbanised countries of Europe must be tending.[21]

FOREIGN WORKERS

A special kind of rural–urban migrant is the foreign worker, on whom the economy of western Europe increasingly relies (Table 6). The countries of the Six currently employ 3.4 million foreign workers, only a million of whom are derived from within the Six, mostly from Italy. Countries of the north and south shores of the Mediterranean are the main sources. Predominantly these workers take over heavy, unpleasant and ill-paid jobs in construction, industry and low-grade service occupations. These jobs are primarily located in industrial cities, where the immigrants are becoming a major element in the population. Problems of adjustment are clearly immense, since the immigrants are simultaneously making the jump into industrial employment, into city living and existence in a foreign country speaking an alien language.[22]

CITY GROWTH IN EASTERN EUROPE

In the planned economies of eastern Europe there have been equally massive changes in the structure of employment. With the exception of a 'western'-type fringe in what is now the DDR, Polish Upper Silesia and the Czech lands, these are countries which before 1945 had an almost colonial type of economy, heavily dependent on primary production, especially agriculture. In Poland, for example, 60 per cent of the 1931 working popula-

30

TABLE 6

European Community (the Six) : Foreign Workers, 1970

Country	From countries of the Six	Total
Belgium	125,000	208,000
Germany	478,000	1,839,000
France	260,000	1,200,000
Italy	12,000	37,000
Luxembourg	26,000	32,000
Netherlands	50,000	110,000
Six	951,000	3,426,000

Source: Commission of the European Communities, *Preliminary Guidelines for a Community Social Policy Programme*, Paper Sec (71) 6oo Final (Brussels, 1971).

tion was employed (it might be more correct to say under-employed) in agriculture, and only 13 per cent in industry. In all these countries there has, since 1945, been a planned and deliberate attempt to change the balance of economic activity, with a privileged position given to manufacturing industry. In Poland the agricultural proportion had by 1960 fallen below 40 per cent, and industry increased to 25 per cent. In the period 1946–62 the industrial work force rose by over 2 millions, or 163 per cent. Other non-agricultural occupations, such as trade, communications and the social services showed correspondng increases. It is only to be expected that these occupational changes have been reflected in a marked increase in the urban population, which in Poland increased by 7 millions in the period 1946–60. Many new centres of industry were created as part of a planned attempt to bring new employment to backward rural areas. The particular encouragement of heavy industry that was characteristic of the period of Stalin's dominance is reflected in the new town of Nowa Huta, which finds its east European parallels in Eisenhüttenstadt (ex Stalinstadt) in the DDR and Dunaujvaros in Hungary. However, the main urban growth came about through the reconstruction and extension of existing cities, and the acquisition of urban status by settlements of rural origin. To take Poland as an example again, the largest absolute increases have understandably been in the largest urban complexes: in 1950–60 a rebuilt Warsaw agglomeration gained 1.6 million inhabitants, Upper Silesia gained 522,000. Nevertheless, proportionate growth was

31

greatest in the medium and small towns.[23] This may reflect a degree of success in Polish attempts to divert growth into backward rural areas, but it no doubt also reflects difficulties in keeping housing provision in the great cities in pace with industrial growth. In any event, similarly rapid growth of medium-sized towns has been noted in western countries, notably France.

As in western Europe also, it certainly cannot be assumed that when an individual changes to a non-agricultural occupation he necessarily moves to live in a city. It has been observed that in 1960 the Polish cities had over 90 per cent of all industrial employment, but contained only 74 per cent of the non-industrial work force. Hundreds of thousands of the workers newly recruited for industry since 1945 have continued to live in their native villages and small country towns, commuting daily to work. Commuting is especially active in the overcrowded agricultural southeast, around Cracow, Nowa Huta and the Upper Silesian industrial region, and also around Warsaw.[24] It has led to a drastic economic and social transformation of villages lying within the commuter zones, and also to their physical transformation by the addition of numerous individual dwellings and the changing of farmsteads into non-agricultural residences.[25] A parallel evolution of commuting appears to have been characteristic of Czechoslovakia.[26]

OTHER DEMOGRAPHIC CONSTITUENTS OF URBAN GROWTH

Cities used to have an evil reputation as 'eaters of men', unable, because of a combination of disease, vice and low birth rates, to maintain their populations without constant transfusions of healthy rural stock. Such a view cannot be reconciled with the fact that today rural–urban migration alone is insufficient to explain the present extent of urban growth. Cities and the city regions around them tend to have lower crude death rates, lower infantile mortality rates and higher crude birth rates than the rural areas around them, and so in consequence have higher rates of natural increase.

The reasons for these contrasts need to be looked at with care. Crude death rates, measured per 1,000 total population, tend to be low in urban areas precisely because these have for the last 30 years or more been the target of migrant flows, and as migrants tend to be younger on average than the populations they leave, so the cities become demographically 'younger', with correspondingly reduced frequency of deaths. The proportion of the aged in the city population is also reduced by the popularity of retirement to rural areas or the seaside. Even when these effects of migration are discounted, urban areas often have a slightly greater expectation of life than rural ones. Presumably this reflects the higher standard of their health services, as no doubt does the tendency for them to have a low infant mortality.

The characteristically high crude birth rates of city regions are similarly the product of immigration, for the age group most likely to move is also the age group that produces children. It is not that women in city regions are inherently more fertile; rather the contrary in fact.

Italy seems to be something of a rule to itself. Its northern city-regions have rates of natural increase broadly equivalent to that of the booming Paris region, although generally below those of the country as a whole. The peculiarity of the demographic pattern of Italy's cities lies in the south, where the ten city regions have rates of natural increase far above those of the country as a whole. Naples is the supreme example, a city-region of 3.5 million inhabitants which owes its continuing growth entirely to natural increase (827,000 in the years 1952–66, of whom 115,000 were lost by net outward migration).[27]

MOVEMENT INTO INDUSTRY

It is a natural assumption that the millions of people moving out of agriculture as an occupation and largely contributing to city growth must have moved into industry. A glance at the table of employment change by major sector (Table 4) shows that this view must be considerably modified. In the countries of the Six industrial employment has been very static in recent years, and even over the longer period 1958–70 net increase has been only about 3 millions, taking the industrially employed active population from 40 per cent in 1955 to 44 per cent in 1970.

The explanation of this unimpressive performance lies in the well-known fact that industry is becoming more and more capital-intensive, and more and more economical in its use of manpower. Labour requirements by no means increase in proportion to the increase in industrial output. The growth rate of industry as a whole is also held back by the enormously contrasting fortunes of its various branches. Some older industries have been going through a profound crisis. Coal in the Six lost 625,000 workers or 60 per cent of its work force between 1958 and 1970. Iron-ore mining, shipbuilding, textiles and leather have also been severely affected. The declining industries are balanced by a group showing conspicuous growth, including chemicals, rubber, machine building, electrical and electronic equipment. Progress has been even more rapid in the motor vehicle and aircraft industries, and most rapid of all in the manufacture of plastics and synthetic fibres.[28]

THE OLDER URBAN–INDUSTRIAL REGIONS

Because these branches of industry are not evenly distributed but tend to cluster in distinctive and often specialist industrial regions, these varying growth rates tend to translate themselves more or less proportionately in terms of varying rates of city growth. One highly characteristic type of urban–industrial region was developed mainly in the years before 1914 on the basis of mining, chemicals based on coal, the smelting of metals and the construction of heavy steam-powered machinery, ships or vehicles, and the machine production of textiles. The older conurbations of Britain, such as Tyneside, Clydeside or the Black Country, were first on the scene; continental equivalents are the Nord region of France, southern Belgium, the Ruhr or Lorraine.

In these older urban–industrial regions, static or declining industries are reflected in static or declining populations, setting them clearly apart from the general European process of urban expansion. The Nord region of France, for example, with its traditional dependence on coal, heavy industry and textiles had a net loss of 33,700 members of the active population in 1962–68 by migration to more fortunately placed regions, and this was in turn reflected in a small migratory loss in the total population. Although this was more than made up by natural increase (fertility rates are, by French standards, high in the Nord) it still left

34

this highly urbanised region with an overall growth rate comparable only with those of really remote rural regions such as Auvergne. We thus see a new type of migration emerging; the growing and successful cities are nourished not only from the countryside and the smaller towns in rural regions, but also from cities of economically less successful regions.

The economic revival of these older urban–industrial complexes is made more difficult by deficiencies in their total environment, produced in the century or more since the onset of industrialisation and urban development. Derelict industrial plants and land devastated by mining are not only visually unattractive but exude an air of failure. A vast heritage of substandard housing is a further depressant. The potential industrialist may also be deterred by the low level of social, educational, cultural and retailing facilities hitherto considered adequate for a predominantly working-class population. He may well be tempted to transfer his interest to another city where success appears to be breeding success, leaving the spiral of degradation in the older urban region to take one further turn for the worse. However, the picture is not one of unrelieved gloom. It is interesting that an area like the Ruhr, fighting back with vigour, has realised that its weapons must include not only the provision of industrial sites but a total upgrading of the urban environment in which new roads, new passenger transit systems, better housing, gleaming new shopping centres, new universities, theatres and parks all have their part to play.

THE INDUSTRIAL BOOM CITIES

The growth of the cities of the older industrialisation in the period up to 1914 radically changed the map of Europe. At a time when transport facilities were less developed than at present, in part even before the railway age, there was a strong tendency for industries to be drawn towards the coalfields, which were the principal sources of energy. New cities, or greatly expanded ones, grew in remote areas, such as Lanarkshire, South Wales, the Saar or the Massif Central, solely because coal was available there.

The new sources of energy that have come to the fore in the present century – oil, natural gas, or the electricity into which primary forms of energy are frequently transformed—are all easily transferred by pipe or cable. Rarely does their utilisation call for the development of new industrial regions and associated urban development. The nearest we come to developments of this kind is the concentration of oil refining and associated petrochemical and power plants at ports and estuaries, at locations where they are often joined by other plants based on imported bulk commodities, such as iron and steel. Rotterdam's Europort and the French port of Fos at the mouth of the Rhône provide the best examples of development of this kind. In general, however, oil, gas and electricity go where they are needed, that is essentially to existing industrial locations, existing cities.

At the same time industry itself has changed its nature. The chain of production has lengthened; only a few initial processing plants are still tied to raw materials, while only the gross consumers are tied to energy sources. One of the strongest locational pulls today is towards labour, not as a rule towards the highly specific skilled labour characteristic of areas like Sheffield or the Potteries in the nineteenth century, but towards large pools of workers accustomed to factory work of any kind. This tends to mean attraction towards the existing large urban agglomerations. Here too are likely to be found the universities, technical colleges and other environmental features that will produce and retain such technologists and managers as may be required.

What is more, as the chain of production lengthens, industrial plants increasingly supply not the final consumer, but other industrial plants. For ease of communication such plants tend to cluster in reasonable proximity to each other, typically in or on the fringe of a great agglomeration. The best known example is provided by the motor industry in centres like Stuttgart or the West Midlands, where the assembly plants must draw thousands of components from tributary plants. These new industries have high rates of growth, which they transmit to the urban areas to which they are attached.

What kind of agglomeration is favoured by these new industries? Not the old heavy industrial regions where these are also in remote locations. The Black Country–Birmingham agglomeration is thus more than acceptable, perhaps also the Ruhr and the Saar, but evidently not Clydeside or Lorraine. The most marked trend is towards the vicinity of great nodal agglomerations which offer substantial labour pools and markets and have good communications with the economically active parts of western Europe. So the present century has seen the marked industrial growth of the traditional regional and national capitals: Milan, Lyon, Frankfurt, Stuttgart or Antwerp, also Paris and London for all but the last few years. Typically, as new plants are attracted, they settle not in the overcrowded core cities but on the fringes of the agglomeration in suburbs and satellite towns. Each new arrival leapfrogs over the one before, drawing in fresh waves of workers, so that the exploding agglomeration explodes still further.

THE TERTIARY SECTOR

In view of the overall decline of employment in agriculture, and the tendency for the increase in industry as a whole to be rather unimpressive, it necessarily follows that all other forms of occupation, falling into what is generally called the tertiary sector, have on balance been expanding with particular rapidity (Table 4). In France, for example, the tertiary sector added 1,260,000 persons in the period 1962–8, three times the increase of industry. In England and Wales in 1951–61, office workers alone increased by 1.2 million or 41 per cent, compared with a general increase for all occupations of 1.6 millions or 8 per cent.[29] It is not just that with generally increasing real incomes the western Europeans are prepared to pay for more of what might be thought of as 'inessential' services, such as better shopping facilities, personal services, air travel or tourism. It is not only the apparently incurable tendency of governments to increase the numbers of civil servants as society becomes more complex and demanding. It is also that the very nature of industry is changing, so that instead of there being just managers and workers, there are now hordes of scientists, designers, market research men, computer experts, accountants, labour relations officers, public relations consultants and the like. All this serves to swell the tertiary sector.

If employment in the tertiary sector were regularly distributed in proportion to the resident population, it would have no impact

37

on city growth. For the most part, however, the service sector is not only urban in location but increases with the scale of the settlement. General stores may be found in villages, but chain stores, supermarkets, general hospitals and comprehensive schools require populations numbered in thousands or tens of thousands to support them, while department stores, teaching hospitals or universities serve populations numbered in hundreds of thousands. The tendency is to place these services in the 'central places', the local, regional and national capital cities that are most easily reached by the population concerned. The high growth rate of the service sector then stimulates further urban growth.

Yet not all agglomerations benefit to the same degree from this expanding sector of the economy. It has already been observed how the older industrial cities, with their static or declining industrial activity, are also poorly endowed with services. In general, the distribution of the growing tertiary sector tends to coincide with that of modern growth industries. Both tend to be attracted to the more accessible of the greater agglomerations, both tend to be under-represented in the older industrial regions.

CHECKING THE GROWTH OF GREAT CITIES

During the period of massive urban expansion since the second world war, most governments in western Europe have made some attempt to limit the tendency for a small number of great city regions, such as north Italy, Paris or southeast England, to grow at the expense of more rural regions and the cities of the older industrialisation. England has a system that combines a strict control over the establishment of new industrial plants in its central area of growth with incentives for industry to locate in the peripheral development areas. It was initially assumed that with the help of these measures the population of the Greater London agglomeration could be held static. By the 1960's it was apparent that London's employment growth rates were continuing to be higher than in the country as a whole. This was partly because London's industrial structure was dominated by the 'new' branches, with an inbuilt tendency to growth. Of much greater significance, however, was the expansion of the tertiary sector, especially office employment, which was for the most part unaffected by the controls over industrial location.

Controls over office building and inducements for office developers to seek sites outside central London were intensified from 1963. No immediate effect was apparent: in 1964–7 the Southeast continued to have half of the newly built office space of England and Wales, and its share of the total continued to increase. On the other hand, by the late 1960's it was apparent that net migration into the region from the rest of Britain and from overseas had fallen to zero, or was even negative, so it may be that the government's measure had had some effect.

France has a parallel system of discouragement of location in the Paris region, and encouragement elsewhere. New industrial and office floorspace in the Paris region can be created only by special permission, and normally involves the payment of special levies. Simultaneously employment is attracted away from Paris by a system of tax advantages, grants and loans accorded to developers. The French government has also attempted to combat the quite extraordinary dominance of Paris in its urban hierarchy by favouring the development of a number of *métropoles d'équilibre* as urban counter-magnets to Paris (Fig. 4). The *métropoles*, cities such as Lille, Marseille or Toulouse, have been made the subject of special regional planning studies, and have been particularly favoured in the allocation of public funds for all kinds of developments. The government has also endeavoured to increase the quality of intellectual life in provincial centres by transferring a number of research and educational establishments out of Paris, greatly to the disgust of those employed in them. There is some evidence that this policy has been successful. The amount of new industrial floorspace created in the Paris region has tended to decline, and in 1962–8 industrial employment fell by 1.1 per cent at a time when in the country as a whole it went up by 6.5 per cent. Results have been less impressive in the tertiary sector, which nevertheless expanded slightly less rapidly than in the country as a whole. In the same period, net population migration into the Paris region showed a marked check, contrasting with the high rate in the period 1954–62.

Fig. 4 France: *métropoles d'équilibre* and some other planning
projects affecting urban regions

The difficulty is to know how much of this differential industrial and urban growth is, in fact, the result of government action,
and how much would have happened anyway as a reaction to
increasing congestion, rising wages and labour shortages in the
growth areas. Western Germany is a country which does not
attempt to limit the establishment of new industries in growth
areas, and where inducements to locate elsewhere tend to be
weakened by the overlapping powers of the Federal government,
the State governments and the local authorities. Even so, whereas
before 1958 new industrial plants were mostly located in the
agglomerations or on their immediate fringes, there has since that
time been a marked swing to locations outside the agglomerations, where labour is easier to find and land prices and taxes are
lower. It would appear that Western Germany is experiencing
rather parallel tendencies in industrial location to those in

France and Britain, without the same measure of compulsion.

However, it would certainly be wrong to think of the new industrial sites as being randomly scattered over rural areas. There is a marked preference for locations within 10 km of a town large enough to offer a range of commercial, administrative and educational services. Where substantial plants are located in German local-government areas with really small populations, these almost invariably turn out to be close to agglomerations or large cities. The pattern of peripheral expansion of conurbations, with tentacles of growth stretching out to embrace neighbouring medium and small towns, is largely confirmed.[30]

4. CITY STRUCTURE

In western Europe the city is not a haphazard collection of buildings of differing age, type and function, but is typically structured into specialised-use zones. The mechanism by which this zonation is produced is primarily economic: national chain stores will outbid all other claimants for sites on busy shopping streets, banks and offices will take possession of the central financial district, and all these uses will outbid housing, which will tend to be expelled from the city centres.

The same economic mechanism operates within the residential quarters, producing a mosaic of housing areas of differing quality. It is as if each intending resident creates his own private map of the city, in which the different zones are ranked according to such attributes as convenience of access, pleasantness of environment, type of property, the presence of particular social groups, or the absence of others. Only the most wealthy can be sure of buying into the part of the city that ranks highest in their estimation. Most others will have to settle for some intermediate point on their private scales of values, according to their means, while the poorest are relegated to the properties that nobody else will touch, forming slum areas, characterised by overcrowding and multiple occupancy.

However, even in the capitalist countries of western Europe the purely economic process of land allocation does not run unchecked. This is partly a matter of time. Because not all leases and tenancies fall in at the same moment, and because, after all, decisions are made by individuals, not all of a select villa quarter will be converted to offices or flats at one and the same moment, not all of a picturesque slum will be simultaneously occupied by trend-setting members of the middle classes. Buildings of an historical or religious nature are likely to be particularly resistant to change; nobody has yet decided that St Paul's will give a higher economic return if torn down to make way for a bank. An even more important check on the purely economic allocation of urban land is provided by the action of central and local government. To varying degrees in the various European countries, historic buildings are protected, building heights restricted, tenants secured against arbitrary eviction, tracts of land withdrawn from the play of market forces by being acquired for municipal housing schemes. To an ever increasing extent governments and city planning departments claim the right to control change within existing cities, and to plan the nature and direction of their growth.

URBAN CORE AND INNER CITY

A standard feature of the city in the western world is the concentration of administrative, financial, commercial, cultural and amusement facilities within a central urban core. Frequently this urban core coincides spatially with the city as it was before the great urban expansion of the industrial age. This inner city is sometimes still defined by its former walls, as at York and Canterbury in this country, or Nürnberg in Germany, and more frequently by the ring of boulevards that have replaced the walls. The typical concentration of these central activities reflects their interdependence. 'Insurance companies as well as banks, lawyers as well as brokers, appear to consider it important to be in one another's environment.'[31]

That these concentrations of central activities coincide spatially with the inner city is in part a matter of inertia: the administration, the exchange, the courts, the central bank, the opera house, the best shops and restaurants tend to be in the inner city because they have always been there. Other activities are attracted to them. Then because most cities have grown concentrically around their historic cores the inner city enjoys the greatest accessibility to the greatest number of inhabitants. This attraction is often reinforced by the typical location of the main railway stations on the ring boulevards encircling the inner city. Normally the urban core becomes dissociated from the inner city only when the latter is particularly inaccessible, in hilltop fortress cities like

43

Edinburgh, Le Mans or Bergamo, or where it became markedly eccentric to the main urban mass, as typically in port cities like Southampton, Portsmouth or Duisburg.[32]

In the larger cities the urban core is itself divided into a number of distinct zones. Accessibility at a central point accounts for the concentration of department and speciality stores, as well as amusement and refreshment facilities. Admittedly centrality in the motor age has too easily caused congestion, leading to the development of peripheral shopping centres, like the vast covered shopping mall of Parly-II, which pays tribute to its location at the gates of Versailles by piping Vivaldi rather than pop into its stores and restaurants. Yet the central shopping districts still have much to offer: all the atmosphere of the big city and, not least, the small specialist shopkeepers and craftsmen who are able to survive in the older properties of the side streets. Nobody who has seen a German city like Hamburg or Nürnberg decorated for Christmas, with stalls on the central squares and along the streets selling anything from fur hats to hot sausages, can doubt that central retailing still has a powerful appeal.

A second distinctive zone is provided by the financial and banking quarter, marked all too frequently by the replacement of historic quarters with characterless office blocks, completely dead at night and dwarfing the relict churches and other historic buildings that recall an earlier community life. Once again, increased congestion, high rents and planning restrictions on building are driving out the larger offices with their massive banks of office machinery to the city fringes. Often a prestige headquarters is left behind in the centre; in Amsterdam, to take but one example, the elegant 17th and 18th century houses along the canals are easily adaptable for such purposes, as well as to accommodate the smaller offices of lawyers, brokers and the like.[33] There may also be a distinct cultural quarter, with institutes of higher education, libraries and publishing house – like the Latin quarter of Paris, with its traditionally active student life. A group of administrative offices usually adjoins the City Hall or Prefecture. In national capitals this expands to a proper administrative quarter, a Via Venti Settembre, a Whitehall or a Wilhelmstrasse. Hotels and restaurants are often found at the main railway station, possibly grouped with a bus station and the

44

town terminal for airline passengers. Some of these zones may be seen on the diagram of the City of Paris (Fig. 5).

All these activities of the urban core are part of the rapidly growing tertiary sector of the economy. With every new department store or office block, more of the inhabitants of the inner city are displaced, to find new homes in the suburbs or beyond.

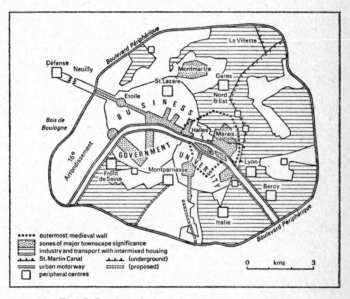

FIG. 5 Structural elements of the City of Paris

Source: Ville de Paris, *Schéma Directeur d'Aménagement et d'Urbanisme de la Ville de Paris* (Paris, 1968).

From there each day the breadwinner must join the tidal flow of commuters, which is one of the consequences of the specialisation of the urban core. Central London, for example, employs 1.3 million workers, of whom only 8 per cent are resident.[34] It is clear that this central concentration of tertiary activities exacts a heavy cost, individual cost in terms of hours wasted in the strained conditions of the journey to work, a public cost in terms of investment in roads and public transport facilities which are fully used

45

only for a few hours of peak travel each working day. Another adverse social aspect is the way in which the city tends to die each evening, since the resident population is so low.

Yet the process of excluding the resident population from the inner city is not everywhere as complete as in the extreme examples of Britain, Scandinavia or North America. Naples is perhaps an extreme case, where five ancient quarters of the inner city house 25 per cent of the total core city population of 1.2 million on a mere 4 per cent of the city area, with densities ranging from 500–800 to the hectare.[35]

To walk the long, narrow 'Spaccanapoli', bisecting the inner city on the line of the Greco-Roman Decumanus Inferior, is to experience a pressure of urban population and a degree of poverty that is otherwise to be met with only in the casbahs of north Africa and the Levant. Rome contains about a quarter of a million people within the walls; in the popular quarters within the bend of the Tiber and across in Trastevere densities reach 700–1,000 to the hectare.[36] In 1962 the Paris inner city (approximately within the ring of the central railway termini) had 950,000 inhabitants, at a density of 351 per hectare. For central Stockholm the figure was 139, and only 100 for central London.[37] Undoubtedly these surviving residential populations bring a life and a liveliness to the inner city that is utterly lacking in the windy spaces around the glass and steel office blocks of the Anglo-Saxon 'central business district'. To see the Piazza Navona on a Rome evening, with the nearby inhabitants taking the air, visiting the pavement cafés, buying from stalls or watching their children play is to appreciate that there are values in city life that may be utterly destroyed by the purely economic process of areal differentiation.

One reason for this higher density is the greater degree of acceptance of living in apartments rather than individual houses, so that the floors above shops in the inner city are residentially occupied, whereas in historic British towns they are all too often left empty. Partly it is a matter of scale. Many cities of continental Europe were so large before the industrial age that the urban core by no means fills the historic inner city: there is room for purely residential or mixed quarters as well. In Nürnberg, for example, the urban core of business streets running through the inner city from the main station to the *Rathaus* and the castle leaves ample space even within the walls for quiet residential quarters that have been rebuilt since wartime devastation.

The most important reason for the continuing residential significance of the inner city is, however, simply that in France and the Mediterranean countries the city is highly valued as a residential location. Nowhere is this more so than in Italy, where even in the Middle Ages the cities, rather than a feudal nobility, were the units of territorial organisation.[38] What is more, the inner city in these countries has not merely a relict population of deprived groups, as sometimes in the Anglo-Saxon world, but is deliberately selected as a prestige residential location by the wealthy. To some extent, indeed, the spatial segregation of the various income groups that is so characteristic of the modern city has yet to work itself out fully in these cities, and the older system of vertical segregation survives. In districts like the Marais, on the east side of the Paris inner city, there are decaying ancient hôtels of the nobility where the entrance courts may now be a clutter of garages and small-scale artisan workshops, but the grand first floors house a diplomat or company director. Then the social scale will be descended with the mounting of every additional flight of stairs, until the students in the former maids' rooms under the tiles are reached. More normally today the inner city is divided socially. Within the inner city of Paris, the wealthier classes have gravitated westwards, towards the Louvre and the government quarters about the Invalides on the south bank (Fig. 5).

There is even a recent tendency for the middle classes to re-occupy areas of high architectural distinction in the inner city, which have passed into working-class occupation or even deteriorated into slums. The process is familiar enough in London, where former Georgian suburbs like Chelsea or Islington have been taken over. It is indeed a welcome spectacle to see some 17th century hôtel in the Marais or on the Ile St Louis stripped of the dirt and accretions of centuries, and restored to its former dignity. Yet the people who can pay for this treatment are inevitably wealthy. In contrast to what is happening in most Anglo-Saxon cities, the centres of cities like Paris or Rome are becoming progressively more middle class as old houses are

47

destroyed or restored and their working-class inhabitants driven out to the edge of the city.

THE MIDDLE ZONE

Wrapped round the inner city is characteristically a belt of high-density housing, mostly the product of the 19th and early 20th centuries. One sector of this middle zone of the city will normally consist of higher income villas and apartments. This higher income sector often grows by prolongation outwards from the pre-existing upper-class segment of the inner city. Alternatively it may be determined by such attractive features as parks, rivers or royal palaces with their gardens. So in Paris we find the fashionable districts of the inner city around the Louvre continued westwards across the Etoile into the 16ᵉ Arrondissement and the southwest part of the 17ᵉ, between the Bois de Boulogne and the Seine, and stretching across the administrative limit of Paris into the suburban commune of Neuilly (Fig. 5). The equivalent in Rome would be the expansion northwards across the walls and the Corso d'Italia, east of the Villa Borghese gardens; in Berlin the former embassy quarter south of the Tiergarten, continuing into Charlottenburg; or (more exceptionally in England) Mayfair and Kensington in London. These 'good' residential districts are normally typified by a high level of equipment in the form of shops, schools, parks, hospitals and clinics. There is a continuing tendency for the parts of these 'good' districts fringing the urban core to be taken over for professional purposes (lawyers, doctors, architects and the like) or for offices. The process is familiar enough in London's Mayfair. The Paris business district has progressively extended on the axis of the Champs-Elysées across the most exclusive residential districts (Fig. 5), while currently there is a great controversy over the invasion of the formerly exclusive Frankfurt 'West End' district by giant office blocks.

Over most of the middle zone, working-class housing predominates. In Berlin and other large German cities this is the zone of the *Mietskasernen* (rent-barracks), five-storey apartments on a maze of airless courts filling the interior of the blocks defined by a rectangular net of wide streets. The equivalent belt in Paris shows greater variation, a mixture of former suburban

48

houses and urban apartments stretching out from the central stations to the edge of the city of Paris, and even beyond into the inner part of the suburban ring. Typical of the middle zone is a large intermixture of industry : medium-sized plants and public utilities on the radiating rail lines and waterways, but more especially hundreds of small plants and independent craftsmen in courtyards and in all sorts of improvised and unsuitable premises. All too often the working-class areas of the middle zone are seriously lacking in facilities, with few open spaces, poor shopping centres, few hospitals and secondary schools, little provision for recreation.

THE SUBURBS

We think of the suburbs as the abode of the middle classes, and this is broadly true in Britain, Germany, Scandinavia and the Netherlands, where the middle classes have long used their mobility and purchasing power to obtain a little more open space and fresh air than is available in the central parts of the city. The middle classes have been followed in their migration by at least the financially more stable members of the working class. Large public housing projects must also seek land in the suburban belt. What is characteristic of the suburbs is segregation. The middle classes tend to move out along what has already become established as the 'good' sector within the inner city and middle zone; to the limited extent that the Parisian middle classes live in suburbs, for example, they mostly lie to the west of the city. Middle-class suburbs are also attracted to pleasant neighbourhoods near rivers, parks or forests : St Cloud and Sceaux in the Paris region, the south-facing plateau slopes overlooking Rouen and Le Havre, Steglitz in Berlin, the banks of the Alster and Blankenese in Hamburg. In an age of greater mobility the middle-class suburbs may also be associated with that new phenomenon, the out-of-town shopping centre, with its surround of vast car parks. One remarkable development can sum up the movement. Parly-II, a suburb for 20,000 inhabitants living in flats, is in the preferred western sector of the Paris region, adjacent to the *Autoroute de l'Ouest* to take commuters to Paris, but also at the park gates of the Château of Versailles. Around the flats are

49

children's playgrounds, tennis courts, swimming pools, a riding stable, landscaped grounds. Down one side of the site is a completely enclosed shopping centre: four department stores, 100 shops, two cinemas, drug store, restaurant, cafés, air conditioning, piped Vivaldi. The shape of things to come?

But Parly-II and the similar 'parks' and 'villages' that are beginning to spread an Anglo-Saxon type of middle-class suburbia along the *autoroutes* leading out of Paris remain something of an exception, although a growing one: the prestige residential area is still the 16ᵉ Arrondissement and adjacent parts of the inner city. In France it is characteristically the working classes who are forced out to the suburbs, which are not the orderly Anglo-Saxon affairs of roses and trim lawns but crowded and unplanned accumulations of often sub-standard individual houses, what the French call *pavillons*. Typically such suburbs are poorly provided with public equipment and services. Much the same is true of Rome, where working-class residents are often relegated to the *borgate*, unplanned peripheral settlements of rudimentary dwellings.[39] In France at least the suburbs have been extended since the second world war by large public housing projects, tall standardised blocks of flats, what the French call *grands ensembles*.[40] The least fortunate of recent arrivals are relegated to the shanty towns, the *bidonvilles*, the *baracche*, squatting on the wastelands in the interstices of the developing agglomeration.

THE RURAL FRINGE

Beyond the suburbs the influence of the city stretches out with diminishing intensity into a zone of commuter towns and villages. In Britain the commuter village is thought of in terms of a colony of ex-urban middle-class residents, of renovated cottages and wives patiently waiting with the car at the nearest rail junction to meet the evening train from town. There are some signs that another type of commuter 'village' may be emerging, developments of small modern houses at prices low enough to be bought by young working-class and lower middle-class families from the cities. In continental Europe the commuter village tends to be a more indigenous phenomenon, its inhabitants derived from the original rural population, workers who have abandoned farming but not their rural residence.

It has been suggested above that the operation of the market in land and buildings has been the prime mechanism for producing the high degree of areal specialisation and social segregation characteristic of the west European city. It should then follow that where, as in eastern Europe, the political system requires direct planning by the state, and accords a minimal role to market considerations, areal specialisation and segregation ought to be sharply reduced. Some evidence that points in this direction is provided by even the most casual visits to east European city centres. East Berlin is perhaps not a particularly good example, since the whole of the war-devastated urban core fell to the lot of the eastern sector, and it is hardly surprising that the capital functions of a country of 17 million people should be something of a misfit within what had once been the nerve-centre of an empire stretching, at its greatest, from the Channel to the Caucasus. Nevertheless, when compared with the bustling cities of the Federal Republic, there is undoubtedly a feeling that life in the urban core is going on at a lower level of intensity, and that consequently the drive for reconstruction after wartime destruction is less urgent. The same appears to be true of the other city centres of the DDR, and this is not entirely surprising in a system where retailing and private trading take very much of a subsidiary position. Even now that the Berlin inner city has been substantially reconstructed as a physical manifestation of the claim that (East) Berlin is capital of the DDR (rather than having a special status like West Berlin), it is apparent that instead of filling the centre with office cliffs the East Germans typically provide for public facilities like shops and restaurants at street level, but build blocks of apartments above. This is also true of the reconstructed centres of provincial cities such as Dresden.

It would appear that the effect of Russian-style socialism upon East German cities has been to reverse the trend to specialisation, and to bring back residential population into the hearts of cities.

51

The same appears to be true of Warsaw, which like many of the East German cities was devastated in the second world war, so that in its rebuilding under the present regime it ought to be possible to see the working out of Russian-type socialist planning principles. It is the impression of one observer that expansion of the central office–shopping core has ceased, and that even the type of retailing has changed.[41] With the growth of everyday shopping facilities in the suburbs, central Warsaw has become an area of specialist, prestige and tourist shops. Much of the industry that was located in central Warsaw before the war has also been relocated in the suburbs and in settlements of the commuter zone. The process is one that is familiar enough in western cities where, however, the land vacated by departing industry would probably have been replaced by office blocks on the expanding fringe of the central business district. In Warsaw the land has instead been used for parks and standard apartment buildings.

The tendency for the east European city centre to grow more, not less, like the city as a whole in its social and economic structure is evidently only one aspect of trends operating over the city as a whole. The high prestige assigned to manufacturing industry in the socialist societies of Russian type has resulted in the dispersion throughout the whole city of large industrial complexes, each with associated housing areas, each of which in turn has appropriate shopping facilities. Because the apartment block is the standard form of housing, the contrasts in population density that previously existed between depopulating centre, 19th-century middle zone and the suburbs with their single family houses have to a very considerable extent been ironed out. So too have social distinctions between the various residential districts. With rents controlled at a relatively low level and uniform for each type of accommodation irrespective of distance from the centre, and with allocation made on social need rather than ability to pay, social segregation has been largely abolished. This is a point that has been made in relation to Prague, at least in the period up to 1960. A housing policy which allocates new dwellings by preference to young families with children, to employees of 'key economic branches' (also often with young children) and to families living in very bad conditions produces a strong correlation between the age of dwellings and the age and household size of their inhabitants. The older the houses, in general, the smaller and older the households living in them.[42]

The effect of this type of housing policy is to produce socially mixed neighbourhoods, with the almost complete disappearance of social status as a differentiating factor. If the situation in East Berlin is any guide, only intellectuals and party leaders of high esteem appear to enjoy anything approaching a distinctive residential area. In general the contrast between centre and suburb is evened out; perhaps the very word suburb ceases to have much meaning. Instead the city is composed of numerous nuclei, in each of which development is of similar intensity. Because of the relative insignificance of the private motor car, the extension of these east European cities is closely related to public transport facilities. In major cities, such as Warsaw, extension follows the suburban rail routes, at first continuously, then in the form of more widely spaced satellite towns and commuter villages, grouped around the railway stations. The green wedges between the radials are less rapidly and completely occupied by housing than in western cities because the lower provision of individual motor transport renders them more inaccessible.

5. COMMUNITY, NEIGHBOURHOOD AND NEW STRUCTURES FOR THE CITY

URBAN RENEWAL

Efforts to make the existing city a better place to live in tend to focus on the middle zone, with its mass of poor-quality housing. Administratively, technically and financially the easiest solution is to sweep away the sub-standard accommodation and rebuild, as in the British slum clearance schemes. Paris is a particularly interesting example where rebuilding is being combined with an attempt to upgrade this run-down environment by the creation of about a dozen new commercial centres (Fig. 5). Apart from some rather soulless building around the Montparnasse Station, two schemes are particularly advanced. In the Fronts-de-Seine operation, 16 residential and office towers are rising from a pedestrian deck 6 metres above ground level, overlooking the Seine. Being situated immediately across the river from the prized 16e Arrondissement, the scheme should have every chance of financial success. More sweeping still is the transformation of the very run-down Italie quarter, where 8,022 dwellings containing 22,000 inhabitants are being demolished, to be replaced by another group of towers, one 200m high, containing 14,000 new dwellings for 50,000 inhabitants, together with substantial amounts of office accommodation. The quarter will be utterly transformed, with the provision of new shopping centres, schools, libraries, swimming pools, sports facilities and open spaces. Eventually it is hoped that the area of renovation will link across the Seine with the redevelopments around the Gare de Lyon and on the site of the wine warehouses at Bercy.

Already these schemes are visually impressive, and they are certainly transforming the public equipment and service provision of the areas concerned beyond all recognition. They are also extremely expensive, only to be financed by drawing in private capital, which means that the apartments are correspondingly highly priced. Those of the original inhabitants with a claim to rehousing are displaced into subsidised blocks on the periphery of each scheme, or to the *grands ensembles* in the suburbs, so that the city of Paris becomes more and more middle class in social composition.

Even where, as with slum clearance schemes in England, the cleared areas are reserved for working-class housing, social problems are not at an end. It is precisely in the middle zone of cities that long-continued working-class occupation has built up strong local community structures, in part as a reaction against the very inadequacy of the environment. Social life typically centres on the streets, with their numerous small shops, pubs or cafés. Chombart de Lauwe, on the basis of studies in Paris,[43] states categorically that the small social unit of the *quartier* is found only in the areas of the city where the standard of living is low.[44] Elizabeth Pfeil, in a classic investigation of neighbouring relations in apartment buildings in industrial Dortmund, stresses the significance of really long residence in building up links.[45] Fifteen years ago Young and Willmott also stressed the significance of the time dimension in the establishment of links of kinship and friendship in the series of 'urban villages' that, at least at that time, made up Bethnal Green.[46] They concluded their study with an appeal for the preservation of the existing dwellings so far as possible, even if this meant forgoing some of the advantages of starting urban renewal with a clean sweep. These principles are at last beginning to be put into effect in Britain. Similar ideas underlie the interesting experiments with the German *Mietskasernen*, which are 'cored' by the removal of buildings in the centre of blocks, to let in light and air and give some green space, while the surrounding apartments are renovated. The process is an expensive one; there must be tedious negotiations with a host of owners and tenants, while in the end between a third and a half of the inhabitants must move away to the suburbs anyway because there is not room for everyone at the higher standard of accommodation.

But can, or should, these intimate neighbourhood structures be preserved? In a study of a clearance area on the edge of the Italie redevelopment scheme in Paris, H. Coing confirmed all that other research workers had discovered about the closeness of relationships in the limited area of the 'quartier', but he regarded this situation as related exclusively to a particularly impoverished type of working-class urban society.[47] To attempt to re-create such close social groupings on redevelopments is, in his opinion, a dream. Even if a significant proportion of the population is rehoused on the spot, which considerably reduces the shock of transition, the move towards new styles of life that has begun with the arrival of television and the motor car becomes irresistible with rebuilding. The inhabitants turn their regard outwards, to live at the rhythm and on the scale of the city as a whole.

STRUCTURES FOR THE SUBURBS

The Anglo-Saxon middle-class suburb is popularly associated with residential segregation according to socio-economic group, with home-centred nuclear families, with anonymity, insecurity and conformity, and with a desperate unattractiveness to the young. Obviously the suburb has its social virtues too, including the opportunities it offers for the development of family life within the home, and a greater amount of neighbourliness than many observers have expected to find. Middle-class people are evidently prepared to work at neighbourliness. 'Sociability becomes a sort of profession', say Willmott and Young of a British middle-class suburb,[48] and much the same point is made about the managerial and professional occupants of *grands ensembles* at Toulouse.[49] Whatever the balance of social advantage and disadvantage, it can at least be said of the Anglo-Saxon suburb that its very newness, coupled with its relatively influential residents, have necessarily caused it to be equipped with a high standard of new roads, schools and other forms of public equipment.

The same can hardly be said of the suburban zones of the cities of France and Mediterranean Europe, with their unplanned individual housing in *pavillons* or *borgate* giving way abruptly to clusters of modern flats or teeming *bidonvilles*. The degree of underprovision can be gathered from the fact that the Paris suburbs lack not only sufficient *lycées*, hospitals or community centres, but even sufficient policemen and police stations, something surely remarkable in a country so centralised and authoritarian as France.

Most European cities have been obliged to develop large peripheral housing schemes for the inhabitants displaced by urban renewal operations, together with the newly married and immigrants. Sometimes these housing schemes become virtual new towns: 25,000 in the Frankfurt Nordweststadt, 50,000 in Buckow-Rudow and other peripheral developments of West Berlin. Although distinguished by a lively architecture, the Berlin developments have been criticised as heartless and lacking the warmth and community feeling of the older districts, but such comments are relatively mild compared with the controversy that has raged around the *grands ensembles*, the French version on the same theme. After 50 years of demographic stagnation, post-war France found itself with a population that was steadily rising and moreover streaming into the cities. The only way in which the construction industry could cope with the new situation appeared to be by building large groups of standardised flats using mass-production methods. The *grand ensemble* was also favoured by many planners on ideological grounds, as a departure from what was considered to be the excessive individualism and isolation of the *pavillons*, in the direction of a more collective form of habitation which, by throwing residents of a variety of social origins into proximity, would create a new classless society.

The earliest plans were admittedly highly uninspiring, composed of rigidly rectangular alignments of identical apartment blocks. Sarcelles, a *grand ensemble* built north of Paris for 55,000 inhabitants, rapidly acquired a national reputation for its real or imagined deficiencies, being denounced as a collection of human rabbit-hutches: cold, impersonal, unfriendly and overpowering in scale. There was no nearby employment, so that the men were faced with a lengthy daily journey to Paris for work, and the women were shut up in their bright new flats to acquire suburban neurosis. In a population where (in 1968) one person out of two was under 20, there was nothing to occupy adolescents, who formed gangs and got into trouble with the police. Communal facilities of all sorts, schools, clinics, shops, municipal offices, community centres, arrived long after the population to be served. Only belatedly have a stadium, a swimming pool, a giant shopping centre and an industrial estate been provided.[50] The same story could, of course, be told of housing projects and new towns in many countries, where it must often seem that the most urgent need is to give people a roof over their heads somehow, leaving other facilities to be provided at a slower pace. Yet enquiries carried out at Sarcelles reveal an overwhelmingly high degree of satisfaction on the part of the inhabitants, who evidently appreciate being well housed in green and peaceful surroundings.[51] Anyone who visits Sarcelles on a Sunday morning now, and sees the main boulevard alive with a long line of colourful market stalls, can believe that what was once a collection of residential blocks is becoming a real town. Not all the initial mistakes of Sarcelles have been repeated in subsequent schemes, but abundant press publicity continues to keep the difficulties of the Paris suburbs before the public eye.

BUILDING NEW SUBURBAN CENTRES

One way to give form and structure to the suburb is by the insertion of new shopping, commercial and administrative centres into the incoherent urban fabric. The Berlin project for a virtual new town of 50,000 population in the Märkisches Viertel is intended to provide shopping, educational and sport facilities for the inhabitants of the surrounding, rather run-down districts as well. The Frankfurt Nordweststadt project, to which reference has been made above, is also intended to 'pull together' a scattered urban fringe population in suburbs and overgrown villages. In Britain, Basildon new town performs a similar function in the sprawling suburbs of south Essex. In this category we may perhaps place the EUR development on the fringe of Rome, a curious collection of monumental museums, ministries, shops and apartment buildings, the somewhat fortuitous product of Mussolini's grandiose plans for a 1942 international exhibition, the 1950 Holy Year and the 1960 Olympics.[52] Unfortunately the proposals in the 1962 Rome plan for the creation of an even

58

greater administrative and commercial centre aligned along the 'Asse Attrezzato', the north–south motorway axis through the eastern suburbs, seems like so many other excellent Italian town-planning proposals to have fallen victim to the twin forces of bureaucratic procrastination and the cupidity of property developers.

Once more the most instructive examples are to be found in the Paris region, where the schemes to provide new centres in the crowded middle zone find their parallels in the more open con-ditions of the suburbs. Where possible the new suburban centres coincide with the Prefectures of the new Departments into which the Paris region has been divided, while office developments and new universities are used to give further social and economic diversity (Fig. 6). The most grandoise of the schemes is the multi-level 'la Défense' project, which is, in effect, a continuation of the Paris central business district (Fig. 5). From a waste land between the proletarian suburbs of Puteaux and Courbe-voie a double line of office and apartment towers surges from a

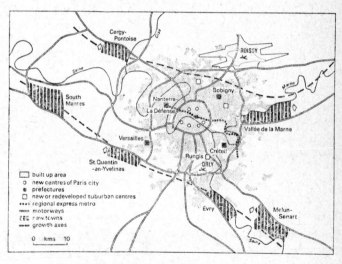

FIG. 6 The *Schéma directeur* of the Paris region

Sources: Principally derived from France, Premier Ministre et Délégation Générale au District de la Région de Paris, *Schéma Directeur d'Aménagement et d'Urbanisme de la Région de Paris* (Paris, 1965).

wide pedestrian deck, giving access to an exhibition hall and shopping centre. Beneath the deck, layer after intricate layer, there are car parks, complex highway intersections, a bus station, the magnificent ticket hall of the new regional express Métro (a shopping and entertainment centre in itself) and, at lowest level, the Métro platforms and tunnels. Just to the west are the Prefecture of the new Hauts-de-Seine Department and the notorious Nanterre *Faculté*, now a university in its own right. A firmer and more authoritative transfer of a run-down area could scarcely be imagined. Less expensive and less advanced, but scarcely less impressive is the development at Créteil, in southeast Paris, where the new Prefecture heaves itself like an ocean liner out of the flooded gravel pits of the Seine–Marne confluence (Fig. 6). A new commercial and municipal centre, a vast teaching hospital and other university buildings are helping to transform what was a very shoddy district indeed. The time may not be so far distant when our stereotyped notions of the depressing nature of the Paris suburbs will have to be revised.

6. PLANNING THE CITY REGION

The greatest influence on urban form today is transport, especially the motor car with its offer of instant, personal, door-to-door movement, and insatiable demands on space. The most intractable problems of planning for the motor car age relate to the heavily built-up areas in the inner city and the middle zone. To what extent should we attempt to adapt this crowded and intricate urban fabric to the demands of the motor vehicle?

Of all the movements of people in cities, the daily tidal flow of commuters into the really large centres is least suitable for movement by car. Some time ago it was calculated that to handle the total commuter flow for the suburbs into the city of Paris would require the building of 40–50 motorways, each with four lanes in each direction, and a quarter of the city would need to be given over for parking space.[53] Not surprisingly this movement is mostly left to public transport, especially the suburban railways. Of the 1.2 million people who travelled to work in central London on each working day in 1966, about three-quarters travelled by rail.[54] Figures for Paris give a proportion of 40 per cent moving by rail, but only 12 per cent by car.[55] Understandably, the tendency to use public transport for the journey to work increases as the size of settlement rises. In France the figure is only about 10 per cent for towns under 10,000 inhabitants, but rises to 56 per cent in the city of Paris.[56] At least in the Paris region the numbers using the suburban railways are increasing, by 23 per cent between 1960 and 1970, obviously reflecting the movement of population out to the suburbs.[57] On the other hand the use of public transport as a whole has recently been declining by $1\frac{1}{2}$ per cent per year, mostly because of the decline of about 4 per cent a year in the use of the buses, which are the principal victims of the congestion caused by increased numbers of cars, the use of which increases by 8 per cent a year.[58]

Rome provides one of the most extreme examples of this unhappy relationship between public and private transport.[59] The city has only one underground railway line, built as a prestige project to give access to the EUR exhibition site south of the city, which, as luck would have it, is in one of the least urbanised and industrialised sectors of the capital. Building the remainder of the net has met with a host of delays – physical, archaeological and bureaucratic. The inhabitants are obliged to use surface transport through the narrow streets of the city, but congestion is so great that speeds are incredibly low, averaging 8 miles an hour, and as little as 3–4 miles an hour in the rush periods. Driven to desperation by the slowness of public transport more and more people turn to the private car which, not being confined to fixed routes, can move a little more quickly than the buses. The result is inevitably to slow down movement in the city even further, while noise, fumes and indiscriminate parking erode the quality of the urban environment. An experiment early in 1971 to reverse the downward trend by offering free travel on the buses failed, since the principal cause of congestion, the private car, remained in possession of the streets.

If in Paris the traffic seems to move a little faster, there is an equivalent degree of congestion. Mercifully, as already noted, only a small number of suburban commuters pass the walls of Paris by car: 92,000 in 1970.[60] But the total number of vehicles of all kinds entering Paris *intra muros* in the course of the day exceeds 800,000, and they join more than 900,000 vehicles registered there. Pressure is such that the morning and evening rush hours are being progressively extended until there is really a single continuous rush from 7 in the morning to 9 at night. An air survey of traffic in the city of Paris made in 1970 showed that only 60,000 vehicles were actually in movement, impeded by 340,000 parked in single or double lines along the roads. A further 440,000 vehicles were parked off the roads, some in surface car parks but many impeding pedestrians by being parked on the pavements.[61] The sheer chaos, frustration and pollution lying behind these figures can be imagined by anyone who knows Paris.

Attempts to meet these problems of extreme congestion by driving new motorways through the city are coming to be looked upon with hesitation. The planners of such roads all too frequently take the line of least resistance through the city's parks and open spaces, which are usually few enough as it is. A prime example is the express highway along the north bank of the Seine, through central Paris, which has destroyed the former peaceful walks along the *quais* and pollutes the whole river with noise (Fig. 5). It seems that this monstrosity is to be duplicated along the south bank, although mercifully the scheme for transforming the tranquil Saint-Martin canal into a north–south motorway through the city appears to have been abandoned.

The alternative to desecrating the open spaces is to drive the motorways through the built-up areas, as Haussmann did with his boulevards, but this may mean the destruction of thousands of homes. Communities are sundered, and the remaining residents battered by the noise of motorway traffic, perhaps thundering round an elevated interchange within a few yards of their windows. Experience also suggests that urban road improvements are promptly filled to capacity by traffic, and congestion rapidly reappears. City residents may well decide that, instead of building a kilometre of motorway to enable more cars to cram into the congested central streets, they would rather (to quote Paris again as an example) have 550 hospital beds, 30,000 primary school places or 800 subsidised flats for the same money.[62]

The process of urban motorway construction would only be completely acceptable if there could be a simultaneous reconstruction of the city, to create peaceful 'environmental areas' turning their backs on their encircling motorways, but an operation on this scale is unlikely to be contemplated, if only on cost grounds. After all, the benefits in terms of traffic capacity are strictly limited. Colin Buchanan's study of a notional reconstruction of a piece of London's West End concluded that 'even given complete and total redevelopment of a central high-density site, there would be a strict limit to the amount of traffic it would accommodate, dictated not so much by its own capacity as by the feasibility of providing a [motorway] network to serve it and all the adjoining areas'.[63]

Faced with such considerations there is a strong temptation to look to measures that are less destructive of the present fabric of the city than the construction of urban motorways. Traffic management schemes can ease the flow of traffic, although not everyone would agree that the sprinting of one-way traffic along formerly quiet back streets makes much of a contribution to the quality of urban living. Measures to control parking can both ease traffic flow and diminish the number of cars entering the city. The difficulty is to persuade motorists to abide by even the most minimal regulations, as any visitor to Rome or Paris can testify. Motor traffic can even be banned altogether from individual streets or even whole areas of the city. The process works best with the narrow shopping streets of the inner city.

The removal of traffic from the Hohe Strasse in Cologne, the rue du Gros Horloge in Rouen or the rue Mouffetard in Paris produces a varied and animated scene that is evidently a great attraction to shoppers and a considerable commercial success. If the motor car is to be reduced or excluded, public transport must be improved. Not all towns are as well provided in this respect as Cologne, where the traffic-free Hohe Strasse extends into a spacious podium around the Cathedral, beneath which are the bus stops and the platforms for the tramway system, now put underground. Nearly every great European city is initiating or extending an underground tramway or railway system, as the one real answer to the problem of the mass transport of people in congested urban areas. Costs are, of course, enormous, and progress correspondingly slow.

Beyond the densely built-up inner zone, the role of the motor car changes. Surveys of the Paris region have shown, not surprisingly, that the proportion of households with a car is greater in the suburbs than in the city proper.[64] The lesser congestion in the suburbs and the difficulty of moving by public transport between one suburb and another (as opposed to radially to and from the city centre) means that the car is much more frequently used for journeys to work, as well as for shopping and social purposes.[65] For lacing together the suburbs and satellite settlements in the city region the motorway comes into its own.

PLANS FOR METROPOLITAN REGIONS

It is the motor vehicle which, above all else, has permitted Europe's urban explosion, this flinging of population far across the countryside around great cities. Provision for movement by motor vehicle has accordingly come to dominate the metropolitan region plans, which are our attempt to bring the explosion under some measure of control. If any common trend can be detected in the sequence of plans for great city regions published since 1944, it is a tendency to move away from the idea of the traditional radial–concentric pattern of the typical city, where congestion inevitably becomes greater as routes converge on the urban core, towards a more open network permitting easy movement in a variety of directions towards a variety of centres of attraction.

The 1944 Abercrombie plan for Greater London had as its basic assumption the belief that London's population could be held stable through controls on industrial employment. Further physical expansion of the agglomeration would be prevented by an encircling green belt, while redevelopment of crowded inner areas would be facilitated by the decanting of a million people to new towns and to other settlements further out (Fig. 7).[66] The new towns have indeed been the greatest achievement of British post-war town planning, but the fundamental Abercrombie assumption of a stable population proved untenable under the impact of a rising birth rate and the rapid growth of office employment. The additional population was obliged to find accommodation as best it could in and around existing settlements within and beyond the green belt. By the time that the situation was reviewed in 1964 it was clear that growth had become a major problem. It was suggested that additional new or expanded towns on a greatly increased scale, new cities in fact, should be established 50–100 miles from central London (Fig. 7). These were to be big enough to acquire a distinct social and economic identity and act as 'counter-magnets' to the attraction of London.[67] Three of these counter-magnets, Milton Keynes new town, Peterborough and a development in Hampshire based on Southampton and Portsmouth, have been retained as features of subsequent plans for the Southeast. It was a logical further development to suggest that since the counter-magnets had in any event to be connected by rail and expensive motorways to central London, it would be desirable to obtain the maximum benefit from these links by developing them into 'corridors' of

65

development (Fig. 7). This interesting proposal, recalling the 'finger' plan for Copenhagen, was not, however, implemented.[68]

Meanwhile, Paris had run through two regional plans in quick succession. The initial PADOG plan (*Plan d'aménagement et d'organisation générale de la région parisienne*) resembled

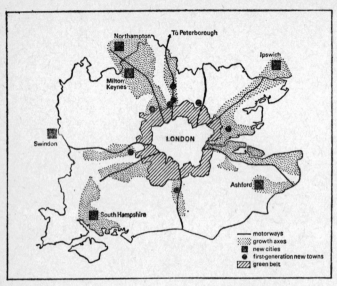

FIG. 7 London and the Southeast: Abercombie and after

Source: Principally derived from UK Department of Economic Affairs, *A Strategy for the South East* (1967).

Abercrombie to the extent that it envisaged freezing the Paris agglomeration at its 1960 limits. Even at the moment of its formal approval the plan was seen to be untenable in the face of the formidable growth of population and mobility in the Paris region. It was rapidly followed by the production in 1965 of the *Schéma directeur*, a much more radical plan.[69] First of all, it advocated the development of new towns, but held that in order to offer an adequate range of facilities they had to be very large, from 300,000 to a million in population, and that to be an effective part of the metropolitan system of Paris they had to be close to the existing agglomeration. Secondly, the existing radial-concentric expansion of Paris had to be checked by aligning these

66

new towns on two great motorway axes parallel to the Seine, and tangential to the existing agglomeration (Figure 6).

The latest of the plans for southeast England has some similarities with the *Schéma directeur*.[70] More indicative and deliberately less precise than former plans, it suggests major growth points based on existing or new settlements which range in population from 500,000 to 1.4 million, and which are thus very much larger than the traditional British new towns. The situation of a large development in South Essex, adjacent to the periphery of London's East End, particularly recalls the Paris proposals. The choice of this location reflects a growing concern with the social implications of regional planning. It has become increasingly apparent that movement to the existing new and expanded towns has been dominated by skilled workers and the more rapidly growing firms. It is now hoped that the shorter movement into South Essex will be within the range of the more disadvantaged workers and the less dynamic firms. The plan also in part mirrors the *Schéma directeur* by attempting to break away from London's radial–concentric pattern, notably by an important diagonal link from the Midlands and the M1 through the expanding towns north of London to South Essex and (presumably) a new Foulness airport (Fig. 8). A shorter tangential link from the M1 would run west of London to link with the new growth areas near Aldershot and in southern Hampshire.

Two of Europe's greatest urban areas require little adaptation to fit in with the most recent ideas of metropolitan region planning. The Ruhr, as a coalfield, has inevitably grown up with a number of distinct nuclei, reflecting the manner in which coal is produced from a number of scattered pits. The physical plan for the Ruhr cleverly uses these characteristics to produce a cellular type of structure, where the settlement nuclei are divided by corridors of open space.[71] A rectangular grid of motorways further defines the cells of the settlement pattern, while the existing road and tramway lines are being developed into a rapid transit system running from centre to centre (Figure 9). The Ruhr plan differs from others in that it does not have to provide for massive population growth, but rather for a radical restructuring of an old industrial region to make it a fitting environment for population and modern industry.

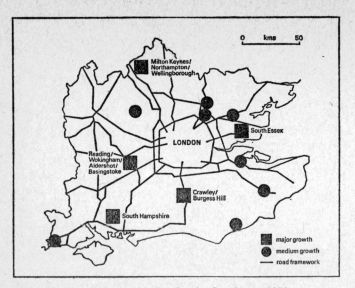

FIG. 8 Strategic plan for the Southeast, 1970

Source: UK Ministry of Housing and Local Government, *Strategic plan for the South East* (1970).

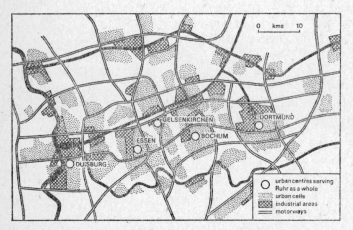

FIG. 9 Structural elements of the Ruhr region

Source: Principally derived from Siedlungsverband Ruhrkohlenbezirk, *Gebietsentwicklungsplan,* 2nd revised edition (Essen, 1970).

Another urban form beloved by the theorists is the linear city, a sequence of centres linked along a single axis, often with a degree of specialisation between one centre and another. An attractive variant is to bend the line back on itself, producing a loop or ring city. The Netherlands *Randstad* has precisely this form.[72] The fact that the western Netherlands consists of a vast polder below the level of the tides has directed urban settlement into a ring round its edge. To an important extent the cities of the ring have specialist functions: Amsterdam for banking and commerce, The Hague for administration, Rotterdam for shipping and industry. Electric railways and motorways link the cities across the green belts that separate them, and across the central 'green heart', which contains the country's international airport. Major expansion is diverted to the outer side of the ring, northwards to the banks of the North Sea canal and the new Ijsselmeer polders, southwards beyond Rotterdam and Europort into the fringes of the Delta.

7. AN URBAN FUTURE?

Will the urban explosion continue, until western Europe is neither pure town nor pure country? There is a kind of Anglo-Saxon dream of the future where distance will be annihilated, where we shall live in a Kentish wood but work in Westminster, hop over to Paris for shopping or Amsterdam for a concert, run down to the coast for sailing or over to Le Touquet for a little golf and gambling. It is clear that this is very much a middle-class vision. We are becoming increasingly aware that modern mobility leaves behind in the decaying cities a highly immobile population consisting of such overlapping categories as the old, the unskilled, the poor and the blacks. There is no real certainty that the situation will be radically different in the year 2001, unless regional planners turn their attention to ensuring that the cities, and not merely the spaces between the cities, provide a fitting environment for people of all classes, incomes and degrees of mobility. This new preoccupation is already evident in the 1970 *Strategic Plan for the South East*. In this process of rethinking our attitude to the city our continental neighbours will at least have the advantage that most of them have never doubted that it is in the city, rather than in the countryside, that life is lived to its fullest extent.

FURTHER READING

Berry, B. J. L., and Horton, F. E., *Geographic Perspectives on Urban Systems* (Englewood Cliffs, New Jersey: Prentice-Hall, 1970), esp. ch. 3 (including a reprinted case-study of urbanisation in Poland by K. Dziewonski).

Blijstra, R., *Town-planning in the Netherlands Since 1900* (Amsterdam: P. N. van Kampen & zoon nv, n.d.).

Burke, G. L., *Greenheart Metropolis: Planning the Western Netherlands* (London: Macmillan, 1966).

Davis, K., *World Urbanization 1950–1970*, vol. 1 (Berkeley: University of California, Institute of International Studies, 1969). Readers should note that this volume consists almost entirely of statistical tables.

Dawson, A. H., 'Warsaw: An Example of Planned City Structure in Free-market and Planned Socialist Environment', *Tijdschrift voor econ. soc. Geografie* 62 (1971), pp. 104–13.

Dickinson, R. E., *The West European City* (London: Routledge, 1962).

Dickinson, R. E., *The City Region in Western Europe* (London: Routledge, 1967).

Hall, P., *The World Cities* (London: Hutchinson World University Library, 1966). The information on the development and planning of major agglomerations given in this book is to some extent brought up to date in:

Hall, P., 'Planning for Urban Growth: Metropolitan Area Plans and Their Implications for South-East England', *Regional Studies* 1 (1967), pp. 103–34.

Hansen, N. M., *French Regional Planning* (Edinburgh: University Press, 1968), esp. chs 2–3, 10.

Heinemeyer, W. F., and Engelsdorp Gastelaars, R. Van, 'Urban Core and Inner City in Amsterdam', *Tijdschrift voor econ. en soc. Geografie* 62 (1971), pp. 207–16.

Hillman, Judy, *Planning for London* (Harmondsworth: Penguin, 1971).

Mayne, R., *Europe Tomorrow* (London: Fontana, 1972, esp. ch. 7 ('The environment') by M. Phlipponneau.

Merlin, P., *New Towns* (London: Methuen, 1971).

Odmann, E. and Dahlberg, G.-B., *Urbanization in Sweden* (Stockholm: Government Publishing House, 1970).

UK Ministry of Transport, *Traffic in Towns* (Buchanan Report) (HMSO, 1963).

UK Ministry of Housing and Local Government *Strategic Plan for the South East* (HMSO, 1970).

Willmott, P., and Young, M., *Family and Class in a London Suburb* (London: Routledge, 1960; N.E.L. Mentor, 1967).

Young, M., and Willmott, P., *Family and Kinship in East London* (London: Routledge, 1957; Harmondsworth: Penguin, 1962).

United Nations, *Demographic Yearbook*, annual. Gives populations on national definitions for capitals and for all cities and agglomerations over 100,000.

NOTES

1. G. L. Burke, *Greenheart Metropolis: Planning the Western Netherlands* (London: Macmillan, 1966).
2. L. Straszewicz, 'Capitals of the Socialist Countries in Europe', *Geographia Polonica* 16 (1969), pp. 27–40.
3. B. J. L. Berry and F. E. Horton, *Geographic Perspectives on Urban Systems* (Englewood Cliffs, New Jersey: Prentice-Hall, 1970), chapter 3.
4. Kingsley Davis (ed.), *World Urbanization 1950–1970*, vol. 1 (Berkeley: University of California: Institute of International Studies, 1969), p. 17.
5. Ibid., pp. 309–14.
6. Maria Kielczewska-Zaleska, 'The Definition of Urban and Non-urban Settlements in East-central Europe', *Geographia Polonica* 7 (1956), pp. 5–15.
7. Straszewicz, *loc. cit.*
8. Révision de la Délimitation des Agglomérations urbaines Utilisées par l'Insee', *Études et Conjoncture* 23(4) (1968), pp. 49–112.
9. G. J. R. Linge, *The Delimitation of Urban Boundaries for Statistical Purposes* (Canberra: Australian National University, 1965), pp. 21–2.
10. S. Cafiero and A. Busca, *Lo Sviluppo Metropolitano in Italia* (Rome: Svimez, 1970).
11. K. Schliebe and H.-D. Teske, 'Verdichtungsräume in West- und Mitteldeutschland', *Raumforschung und Raumordnung* 27 (1969), pp. 145–56.
12. 'Stadtregionen in der Bundesrepublik Deutschland', *Forschungs- und Sitzungsberichte der Akademie für Raumforschung und Landesplanung* 14 (Bremen, 1960). 'Stadtregionen in der Bundesrepublik Deutschland, 1961', *Forschungs- und Sitzungsberichte der Akademie für Raumforschung- und Landesplanung* 32 (Hanover, 1967).
13. Kingsley Davis, *et al.*, *The World's Metropolitan Areas* (Berkeley: University of California Press, 1959). Davis, *World Urbanization 1950–1970*, vol. 1 (Berkeley: University of California, Institute of International Studies, 1969).

14. Commission of the European Communities, *Preliminary Guidelines for a Community Social Policy Programme*, Document Sec (71) 600 Final (Brussels, 1971), pp. 9–17.
15. S. H. Franklin, *Studies in Contemporary Europe: Rural Societies* (London: Macmillan, 1971), pp. 24–5.
16. P.-A. Muet and P. Bolton, 'Evolution de l'Emploi dans les Régions', *Les Collections de l'Insee* R4, 1970.
17. M. Schiray and P. Elie, 'Les Migrations entre Régions et au Niveau Catégories de Commune de 1954 à 1962', *Les Collections de l'Insee* D4, 1970.
18. 'Statistiques et Indicateurs des Régions françaises, 1970', *Les Collections de l'Insee* R7, 1971.
19. Cafiero and Busca, *op. cit.*, Table 4.
20. K. Schwarz, 'Neuere Tendenzen der regionalen Bevölkerungsentwicklung', *Raumforschung und Raumordnung* 25 (1967), pp. 145–54.
21. UK Office of Population Censuses and Surveys, *Census 1971, England and Wales, Preliminary Report*.
22. Commission of the European Communities, *op. cit.*, pp. 18–27.
23. K. Dziewónski and L. Kosiński, 'Changes in the Distribution of Population in Poland in 1950–1960', *Geographia Polonica* 7 (1965), pp. 69–79.
24. T. Lijewski, 'Overpopulation in Agriculture and the Localization of New Industrial Centres in Poland', *Geographia Polonica* 7 (1965), pp. 107–14.
25. Maria Dobrowolska and J. Rajman, 'Socio-economic Structure and Dynamics of the Suburban Zone', *Geographia Polonica* 7 (1965), pp. 115–32.
26. Kielczewska-Zaleska, *loc. cit.*
27. Cafiero and Busca, *loc. cit.*
28. Commission of the European Communities, *op. cit.*, ch. 2.
29. UK Ministry of Housing and Local Government, *Strategic Plan for the South East* (HMSO, 1970), paragraph 2.11.
30. G. Müller, 'Tendenzen regionaler Industrieentwicklung', *Raumforschung und Raumordnung* 25 (1967), pp. 111–18.
31. W. F. Heinemeyer and R. van Engelsdorp Gastelaars, 'Urban Core and Inner City in Amsterdam', *Tijdschrift voor econ. en soc. Geografie* 62 (1971), pp. 207–16.
32. Erika Wagner and G. Ritter, 'Zur Stadtgeographie von Duisburg', *Duisburger Hochschul beiträge* 1 (1968).
33. Heinemeyer and Van Engelsdorp Gastelaars, *loc. cit.*
34. UK Ministry of Housing and Local Government, *op. cit.*, paragraph 2.29.

35. M. Coquery, 'Aspects démographiques et Problèmes de Croissance d'une Ville "Millionaire": Le Cas de Naples', *Annales de Géographie* 72 (1963), pp. 572–604.
36. La Documentation française, 'Les Grandes Villes du Monde: Rome', *Notes et Études documentaires* (Paris, 1970), 3,694–5.
37. 'Paris et Huit Métropoles mondiales', *Cahiers de l'Institut d'Aménagement et d'Urbanisme de la Région Parisienne* 2 (1965).
38. Dominique Schnapper, *L'Italie rouge et noire: Les Modèles culturels de la Vie quotidienne à Bologne* (Paris, 1971), ch. 3.
39. F. Ferrarotti, *Roma da Capitale a Periferia*, 2nd edition (Bari, 1971).
40. P. Clerc, *Grands Ensembles, Banlieues nouvelles* (Paris, 1967).
41. A. H. Dawson, 'Warsaw: An Example of Planned City Structure in Free-Market and Planned Socialist Environment', *Tijdschrift voor econ. en soc. Geografie* 62 (1971), pp. 104–13. Mr Dawson's interesting paper is the sole source of the information on the growth patterns of Warsaw given in this section.
42. J. Musil, 'The Development of Prague's Ecological Structure', in R. E. Pahl (ed.), *Readings in Urban Sociology* (Oxford: Pergamon, 1968) pp. 232–59.
43. P. H. Chombart de Lauwe *et al.*, *Paris et l'Agglomeration Parisienne* (Paris, 1952), chs. 8 and 10.
44. P. H. Chombart de Lauwe, *Des Hommes et des Villes* (Paris, 1963), ch. 2.
45. E. Pfeil, 'The Pattern of Neighbouring Relations in Dortmund-Nordstadt', in Pahl, *Readings in Urban Sociology*, pp. 136–58.
46. M. Young and P. Willmott, *Family and Kinship in East London* (London: Routledge, 1957; Harmondsworth: Penguin, 1962).
47. H. Coing, *Rénovation urbaine et Changement social* (Paris, 1966).
48. P. Willmott and M. Young, *Family and Class in a London Suburb* (London: Routledge, 1960; N.E.L. Mentor, 1967), ch. 11.
49. R. Ledrut, *L'Espace social de la Ville* (Paris, 1968), ch. 2.
50. J. Duquesne, *Vivre à Sarcelles?* (Paris, 1966).
51. *Le Monde*, 2 October, 1968.
52. I. Insolera, *Roma Moderna* (Turin, 1962).
53. P. Merlin, *Les Transports Parisiens* (Paris, 1967), p. 434.
54. UK Ministry of Housing and Local Government, *op. cit.*, paragraph 6.22.
55. 'Evolutions des Migrations alternantes', *Cahiers de l'Institut d'Aménagement et l'Urbanisme de la Région Parisienne* 4–5 (1966).
56. A. Villeneuve, 'Les Déplacements domicile–travail', *Economie et Statistique* 17 (1970), pp 3–16.
57. *Le Monde*, 30 November, 1971.

58. *Le Monde*, 24 April, 1971.
59. La Documentation française, *op. cit.*, pp. 51–9.
60. Villeneuve, *op. cit.*, p. 8.
61. Statement by Prefect of Police as reported in *Le Monde*, 16 January, 1971.
62. *Le Monde*, 24 March, 1971.
63. UK Ministry of Transport, *Traffic in Towns* (Buchanan Report) (HMSO, 1963), p. 142.
64. 'Déplacements de Personnes en Région Parisienne', *Cahiers de l'Institut d'Aménagement et l'Urbanisme de la Région Parisienne* 17–18 (1969), pp. 7–8.
65. Villeneuve, *loc. cit.*
66. P. Abercrombie, *Greater London Plan, 1944* (London: HMSO, 1945).
67. UK Ministry of Housing and Local Government, *The South East Study* (HMSO, 1964).
68. UK Department of Economic Affairs, *A Strategy for the South East* (HMSO, 1967).
69. France, Premier Ministre et Délégation Générale au District de la Région de Paris, *Schéma directeur d'Aménagement et d'Urbanisme de la Région de Paris* (Paris, 1965).
70. UK Ministry of Housing and Local Government, *Strategic Plan for the South East*.
71. Siedlungsverband Ruhrkohlenbezirk, *Gebietsentwicklungsplan*, 2nd revised edition (Essen, 1970).
72. Burke, *op. cit.*

INDEX

Abercrombie, Sir Patrick, 65
administrative quarter, 43, 44,
Fig. 5
Amsterdam, 10, 44, 69, Fig. 2,
Table 2
Antwerp, 37
Austria, 12, 20, Table 3

baracche, 50
Belgium, 12, 23
Belgrade (Beograd), 17, 23
Bergamo, 44
Berlin
industry, 49
size, 19, Fig. 3
structure, 48–9, 57
urban renewal, 55
East, 51, 53
Bethnal Green, 55
bidonvilles, 50, 56
Birmingham, 10, 12, 36,
Fig. 2, Table 2. *See also*
West Midlands
Black Country, 34, 36. *See also*
West Midlands
borgate, 50, 56
Bratislava, 17
Brno, 17
Brunswick (Braunschweig), 12
Brussels (Brussel, Bruxelles),
Fig. 2, Table 2
Buchanan, Sir Colin, 63
Bucharest (Bucureşti), 19, 23,
Fig. 3

Budapest, 17, Fig. 3
Bulgaria, 17, Table 3

Canterbury, 43
central business district, 44–5,
48, 52, Fig. 5
central places 24, 38
Charlottenburg, 48
Chelsea, 47
Cluj, 17
Clydeside, 34, 36
coalfields, 12, 34, 35
Cologne (Köln), 10, 64,
Table 2
commuter villages, 25–6, 32,
50–1, 53
commuting, 24, 32, 45, 61–2
Copenhagen (Köbenhavn), 12
Cracow (Kraków), Fig. 3
Créteil, 60, Fig. 6
cultural quarter, 44, Fig. 5
Czechoslovakia, 16–17, 23,
Table 3

Défense, La, 59–60, Figs.
5 and 6
Denmark, 13, Table 3
Düsseldorf, 10, Table 2

Edinburgh, 44
EUR (Esposizione Universale),
Rome, 58, 62

financial quarter, 44. *See also* central business district
foreign workers, 29, 30, Table 6
France
  cities, 10–12
  city definition, 21–3
  city growth, 26–9
  city size, 17–19, Fig. 2
Frankfurt, 11, 37, 48, 57, Fig. 2, Table 2. *See also* Rhine–Main region
Fronts-de-Seine (Paris), 54, Fig. 5

Germany, Democratic Republic, 16, 51, Table 3
Germany, Federal Republic
  cities, 10–12
  city definition, 22–3
  city growth, 29–30
  city size, 17, 19, Fig. 2
  urbanisation, 13, Table 3
grands ensembles, 50, 55, 57–8

Hague, The ('s Gravenhage), 10, 69
Hamburg, 12, 44, 49, Fig. 2, Table 2
Hanover (Hannover), 12, 22, Table 2
Heidelberg, 11. *See also* Rhine–Neckar region
Hungary, 17, 22–3, Table 3

Iaşi, 17
industry, 33–41, 47, 48, 52
inner city, 43–8, Fig. 5
Ireland, 20, Table 3
Italie quarter (Paris), 54, 55–6, Fig. 5

Italy, 21, 23, 29, 33, Table 3

journey to work, *see* commuting
Jugoslavia, 17, Table 3

Katowice–Bytom–Zabrze, 19, Fig. 3

Le Mans, 44
Le Marais, 47, Fig. 5
Limousin region, 29
Lisbon (Lisboa), 12
Lodz, Fig. 3
London
  city size, 19, Fig. 2, Table 2
  commuting, 61
  industry, 37
  metropolitan region plans, 65–7
  office development, 38–9, 48
  population, 10, 12, 17, 46
  structure, 46–8
  tertiary sector, 38–9
Lorraine region, 34, 36
Lyon, 10, 18, 37, Fig. 2, Table 2

Mannheim, 11. *See also* Rhine–Neckar region
Marseille, 10, 12, 18, Table 2
métropoles d'équilibre, 39, Fig. 4
metropolitan region plans, 61–70, Figs. 6–9
Mezzogiorno, 29
middle zone of cities, 48–9, 54
Mietskasernen, 48, 55
Milan (Milano), 37, Fig. 2, Table 2
Milton Keynes, 65, Figs. 7–8

motorways, 62–4, 66–7
Munich (München), 22, Fig. 2,
   Table 2

Nanterre, 60, Fig. 6
Naples (Napoli) 12, 33, 46,
   Table 2
neighbourhoods, 55–6
Netherlands, 10, 13, 20–1,
   Table 3
new towns, 65–7
Nord region (France), 10, 34,
Nuremberg (Nürnberg), 43, 44,
   46, Table 2

office development, 37–9,
   43–5, 48

Paris
   business district, 39, 59
   city size, 19, Fig. 2
   commuting, 61–2
   industry, 37, 47, 48
   motorway schemes, 62–4
   office development, 39
   population, 10, 12, 17, 21–2,
      26–9, 46, Table 2
   structure, 44–50, Figs. 5
      and 6
   tertiary sector, 39
   transport, 61–4
   urban renewal, 54–60, Fig. 5
Parly-II, 44, 49–50
pavillons, 50, 56
pedestrian precincts, 64
Poland, 16, 22, 30–2, Table 3
population, 10–25, 25–41, 32–3
Portsmouth, 44, 65
Prague (Praha), 17, 23, 52,
   Fig. 3

Provence–Côte d'Azur region,
   26, 29

Randstad (Netherlands), 10, 69
retailing, 44, 50, 52
Rhine–Main region, 11
Rhine–Neckar region, 11,
   Table 2
Rhine–Ruhr region, 10, 12
   Table 2
Rhône–Alps region, 26, 29
Rome (Roma)
   city size, Fig. 2
   growth, 29
   population, 46, Table 2
   structure, 46–50
   transport, 61–2
Rotterdam, 10, 36, 69, Table 2
Rouen, 22, 49, 64
Ruhr
   city size, 18
   industry, 36
   population, 10, 12, 17,
      Fig. 2, Table 2
   regional plan, 35, 67, Fig. 9
   See also Rhine–Ruhr region
Rumania, 17, Table 3

Saar, 35, 36
Sarcelles, 57–8
shopping centres, 44, 49
slum clearance, 55–6
Sofia, 17, 23, Fig. 3
Southampton, 12, 44, 65
Southeast England, 10, 65–7,
   Figs. 7 and 8
Spain, 12, Table 3
Stockholm, 46
Stuttgart, 11, 36, Fig. 2, Table
   2
suburban centres, 58–60

suburbs, 49–50, 56–60, 61, 64
Switzerland, 11, 20, 23, Table 3

tertiary sector, 37–41, 43–6, 48
traffic management, 63–4
transport, 45–6, 53, 61–4
Tyneside, 34, Table 2

United Kingdom
  cities, 10
  city definition, 20, 23
  city growth, 30
  city size, 19, Fig. 2,
  commuter villages 50
  urban renewal, 54–6
  urbanisation, 13, Table 3
urban core, 43–8, 52, Fig. 5

urban renewal, 54–6
urbanisation, degree of,
  12–17, Table 3

Vienna (Wien), 12, Fig. 2,
  Table 2

Warsaw (Warszawa), 19, 31–2,
  52–3, Fig. 3
West Midlands, 36

York, 43

Zagreb, 17
Zürich, 18, Fig. 2

STUDIES IN CONTEMPORARY EUROPE

In the past quarter of a century European society, and Europe's relations with the rest of the world, have been radically transformed.

Some of these changes came in the wake of the Second World War; others – and in particular the division of Europe – followed as a result of the Cold War. In addition, throughout the period other forces, and especially technological change, have been at work to produce a major recasting of the fabric of European society and Europe's role in the world. Many of these changes, together with their attendant problems, have transcended the political and economic divisions of the continent.

The purpose of this series is to examine some of the major economic, social and political developments of the past twenty-five years in Europe as a whole – both East and West – considering the problems and opportunities facing Europe and its citizens today.

STUDIES IN CONTEMPORARY EUROPE

General Editors: ROY PRYCE *and* CHRISTOPHER THORNE

Published titles

AGRICULTURE	HUGH D. CLOUT
THE URBAN EXPLOSION	T. H. ELKINS
RURAL SOCIETIES	S. H. FRANKLIN
YOUTH AND SOCIETY	F. G. FRIEDMANN
THE MASS MEDIA	STUART HOOD
THE QUEST FOR GROWTH	MICHAEL SHANKS
EDUCATION	JOHN VAIZEY

THE URBAN
EXPLOSION

T. H. ELKINS

*Dean of the School of European Studies and Professor of Geography,
University of Sussex*

MACMILLAN

First published *1973* by
THE MACMILLAN PRESS LTD
London and Basingstoke
Associated companies in New York Toronto
Dublin Melbourne Johannesburg and Madras

SBN 333 12151 1

Printed in Great Britain by
THE ANCHOR PRESS LTD
Tiptree, Essex

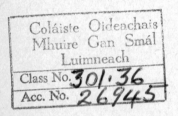